MW00334432

PSSA

Math workbook

3rd Grade Math Exercises, Activities, and Two Full-Length PSSA Math Practice Tests

By

Michael Smith & Reza Nazari

PSSA Math Workbook

Published in the United State of America By

The Math Notion

Email: info@Mathnotion.com

Web: www.MathNotion.com

Copyright © 2019 by the Math Notion. All rights reserved. No part of this publication may be reproduced, stored in a retrieval system, or transmitted in any form or by any means, electronic, mechanical, photocopying, recording, scanning, or otherwise, except as permitted under Section 107 or 108 of the 1976 United States Copyright Ac, without permission of the author.

All inquiries should be addressed to the Math Notion.

About the Author

Michael Smith has been a math instructor for over a decade now. He holds a master's degree in Management. Since 2006, Michael has devoted his time to both teaching and developing exceptional math learning materials. As a Math instructor and test prep expert, Michael has worked with thousands of students. He has used the feedback of his students to develop a unique study program that can be used by students to drastically improve their math score fast and effectively.

- **SSAT Math Workbooks**
- **ISEE Math Workbooks**
- **ACT Aspire Math Workbooks**
- **SBAC Math Workbooks**
- **Common Core Math Workbooks**
- **many Math Education Workbooks**
- **and some Mathematics books …**

As an experienced Math teacher, Mr. Smith employs a variety of formats to help students achieve their goals: He tutors online and in person, he teaches students in large groups, and he provides training materials and textbooks through his website and through Amazon.

You can contact Michael via email at:

info@Mathnotion.com

PSSA Math Workbook

PSSA Math Workbook reviews all PSSA Math topics and provides students with the confidence and math skills they need to succeed on the PSSA Math. It is designed to address the needs of PSSA test takers who must have a working knowledge of basic Mathematics.

This comprehensive workbook with over 2,500 sample questions and 2 complete PSSA tests can help you fully prepare for the PSSA Math test. It provides you with an in-depth focus on the math portion of the exam, helping you master the math skills that students find the most troublesome. This is an incredibly useful tool for those who want to review all topics being covered on the PSSA Math test.

PSSA Math Workbook contains many exciting features to help you prepare for the PSSA Math test, including:

- Content 100% aligned with the 2019-2020 PSSA test
- Provided and tested by PSSA Math test experts
- Dynamic design and easy-to-follow activities
- A fun, interactive and concrete learning process
- Targeted, skill-building practices
- Complete coverage of all PSSA Math topics which you will be tested
- 2 full-length practice tests (featuring new question types) with detailed answers.

The only prep book you will ever need to ace the PSSA Math Test!

WWW.MathNotion.COM

… So Much More Online!

✓ FREE Math Lessons

✓ More Math Learning Books!

✓ Mathematics Worksheets

✓ Online Math Tutors

For a PDF Version of This Book

Please Visit WWW.MathNotion.com

Contents

Chapter 1: Numbers, Comparing and Patterns

Topics that you'll learn in this chapter:

- ✓ Odd or Even

- ✓ Number Sequences

- ✓ Roman Numerals

- ✓ Word Names for Numbers

- ✓ Comparing and Ordering Numbers

- ✓ Repeating Pattern

- ✓ Growing Patterns

- ✓ Place Values

- ✓ Ordinal Numbers

Odd or Even

✎Identify whether each number is even or odd.

1) 38 _____

2) 25 _____

3) 53_____

4) 78 _____

5) 49 _____

6) 87 _____

7) 74 _____

8) 55 _____

9) 98 _____

10) 26 _____

11) 10 _____

12) 90 _____

✎Circle the even number in each group.

13) 83, 27, 23, 15, 33, 48

14) 95, 47, 56, 11, 87, 63

15) 27, 59, 26, 41, 33, 93

16) 13, 88, 99, 55, 79, 53

17) 11, 64, 99, 3, 57, 87

✎Circle the odd number in each group.

18) 38, 4, 14, 82, 63, 50

19) 40, 52, 76, 99, 84, 16

20) 72, 88, 26, 15, 24, 10

21) 12, 94, 52, 68, 41, 76

22) 8, 50, 78, 35, 94, 36

Number Sequences

Write the next three numbers in each counting sequence.

1) $-42, -26, -10,$ ___, ___, ___, ___

2) $285, 242, 199,$ ___, ___, ___, ___

3) $26, 33,$ ___, ___, ___, 61

4) $37, 44,$ ___, ___, $65,$ ___

5) $52, 61,$ ___, ___, ___

6) $87, 75,$ ___, ___, ___

7) $98, 75, 52,$ ___, ___, ___

8) $-52, -33, -14,$ ___, ___, ___

9) $-155, -125, -95,$ ___, ___, ___

10) $-300, -200, -100,$ ___, ___, ___

11) What are the next three numbers in this counting sequence?

$$750; 1{,}100; 1{,}450; \underline{\quad}; \underline{\quad}; \underline{\quad}$$

12) What is the fifth number in this counting sequence?

$$13, 21, 29, \underline{\quad}$$

13) What is the eighth number in this counting sequence?

$$8, 19, 30, \underline{\quad}$$

Roman Numerals

1	I	11	XI	21	XXI
2	II	12	XII	22	XXII
3	III	13	XIII	23	XXIII
4	IV	14	XIV	24	XXIV
5	V	15	XV	25	XXV
6	VI	16	XVI	26	XXVI
7	VII	17	XVII	27	XXVII
8	VIII	18	XVIII	28	XXVIII
9	IX	19	XIX	29	XXIX
10	X	20	XX	30	XXX

✍ Write in Romans numerals.

1) 4 _____   6) 22 _____

2) 8 _____   7) 17 _____

3) 16 _____   8) 11 _____

4) 25 _____   9) 28 _____

5) 18 _____   10) 13 _____

11) Add 4 + 5 and write in Roman numerals.   _____

12) Add 5 + 17 and write in Roman numerals.   _____

13) Subtract 15 – 3 and write in Roman numerals. _____

14) Subtract 25 – 9 and write in Roman numerals. _____

Write Numbers in Words

✍ Write each number in words.

1) 743 _____

2) 275 _____

3) 860 _____

4) 925 _____

5) 483 _____

6) 206 _____

7) 4,717 _____

8) 8,444 _____

9) 5,012 _____

10) 10, 139 _____

11) 1,670 _____

12) 2,390 _____

13) 1,001 _____

14) 7,777 _____

Comparing and Ordering Numbers

✎ Use less than, equal to or greater than.

1) 59 _____ 61

2) 93 _____ 96

3) 96 _____ 69

4) 32 _____ 23

5) 67 _____ 67

6) 26 _____ 16

7) 66 _____ 56

8) 25 _____ 17

9) 68 _____ 68

10) 90 _____ 100

11) 61 _____ 74

12) 79 _____ 49

13) 49 _____ 46

14) 105 _____ 110

✎ Order each set numbers from least to greatest.

15) $-11, -20, 15, -23, 8$ ___, ___, ___, ___, ___, ___

16) $5, -7, 7, -5, 0$ ___, ___, ___, ___, ___, ___

17) $18, -32, 35, -1, -15$ ___, ___, ___, ___, ___, ___

18) $29, -84, 2, -69, -41$ ___, ___, ___, ___, ___, ___

19) $-26, -62, 65, -35, -64, -54$ ___, ___, ___, ___, ___, ___

20) $86, 8, 69, 96, 87, 54, 45$ ___, ___, ___, ___, ___, ___

Repeating Pattern

✎ Circle the picture that comes next in each picture pattern.

1)	◆ ▲ ◆ ▲	◆ ▲
2)	⬠ ◆ ◆ ⬠	◆ ⬠
3)	✶ ⬭ ✶ ⬭ ✶	✶ ⬭
4)	♥ ☺ ☺ ♥	☺ ♥
5)	● ✶ ✶ ●	✶ ●

Growing Patterns

✏️ Draw the picture that comes next in each growing pattern.

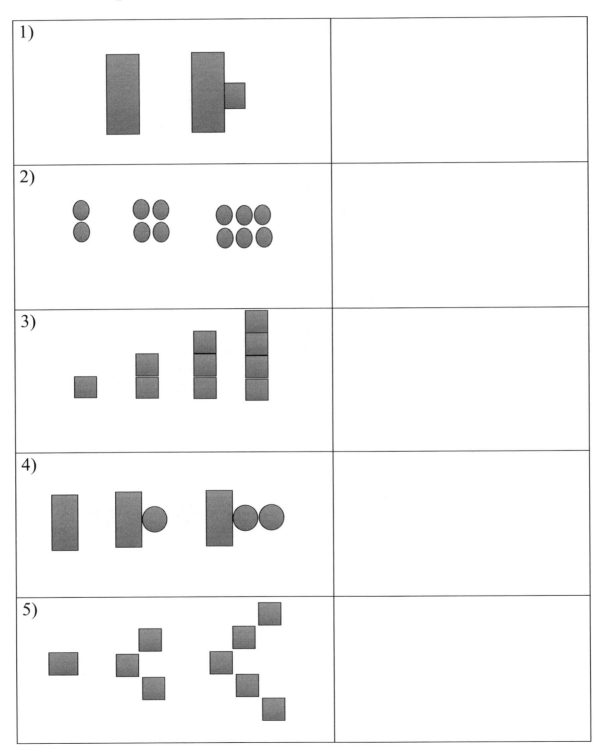

Place Values

✎ Write numbers in expanded form.

1) Fifty –eight   ___ + ___

2) Sixty –nine   ___ + ___

3) Twenty –one   ___ + ___

4) eighty–four   ___ + ___

5) Thirty –seven   ___ + ___

Circle the correct choice.

6) The 1 in 41 is in the

                     ones place   tens place   hundreds place

7) The 5 in 156 is in the

                     ones place   tens place   hundreds place

8) The 8 in 891 is in the

                     ones place   tens place   hundreds place

9) The 3 in 936 is in the

                     ones place   tens place   hundreds place

10) The 4 in 413 is in the

                     ones place   tens place   hundreds place

Ordinal Numbers

✍ Identify the ordinal position of the letters.

1) D   _____

2) E   _____

3) H   _____

4) M   _____

5) W   _____

6) J   _____

7) N   _____

8) S   _____

9) U   _____

10) K   _____

✍ Write the months in ordinal numbers.

11) September is the   _____

12) June is the   _____

13) April is the   _____

14) March is the   _____

Answers of Worksheets – Chapter 1

Odd or Even

1) even

2) odd

3) odd

4) even

5) odd

6) odd

7) even

8) odd

9) even

10) even

11) even

12) even

13) 48

14) 56

15) 26

16) 88

17) 64

18) 63

19) 99

20) 15

21) 41

22) 35

Patterns

1) 6, 22, 38

2) 156, 113, 70

3) 40, 47, 54

4) 51, 58, 72

5) 70, 79, 88

6) 63, 51, 39

7) 29, 6, – 17

8) 5, 24, 43

9) −65, −35, −5

10) 0, 100, 200

11) 1,800; 2,150; 2,500

12) 45

13) 85

Roman Numerals

1) IV

2) VIII

3) XVI

4) XXV

5) XVIII

6) XXII

7) XVII

8) XI

9) XXVIII

10) XIII

11) IX

12) XXII

13) XII

14) XVI

Word Names for Numbers

1) seven hundred forty-three

2) two hundred seventy-five

3) eight hundred sixty

4) nine hundred twenty-five

5) four hundred eighty-three

6) two hundred six

7) four thousand, seven hundred seventeen

8) nine thousand, four hundred forty-four

9) five thousand, twelve

10) ten thousand, one hundred thirty-nine

11) one thousand, six hundred seventy

12) two thousand, three hundred ninety

13) one thousand, one

14) seven thousand, seven hundred seventy-seven

Comparing and Ordering Numbers

1) 59 less than 61

2) 93 less than 96

3) 96 greater than 69

4) 32 greater than 23

5) 67 equals to 67

6) 26 greater than 16

7) 66 greater than 56

8) 25 greater than 17

9) 68 equals to 68

10) 90 less than 100

11) 61 less than 74

12) 79 greater than 49

13) 49 greater than 46

14) 105 less than 110

15) $-23, -20, -11, 8, 15$

16) $-7, -5, 0, 5, 7$

17) $-32, -15, -1, 18, 35$

18) $-84, -69, -41, 2, 29$

19) $-64, -62, -54, -35, -26, 65$

20) $8, 45, 54, 69, 86, 87, 96$

Repeating pattern

1)

2)

3)

4)

5)

Growing patterns

1)

2)

3)

4)

5)

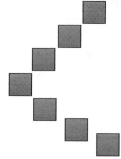

Place Values

1) 50 + 8

2) 60 + 9

3) 20 + 1

4) 80 + 4

5) 30 + 7

6) ones place

7) tens place

8) hundreds place

9) tens place

10) hundreds place

Ordinal numbers

1) fourth

2) fifth

3) eighth

4) thirteenth

5) twenty-third

6) tenth

7) fourteenth

8) nineteenth

9) twenty-first

10) eleventh

11) 9th month of the year

12) 6th month of the year

13) 4th month of the year

14) 3th month of the year

Chapter 2:

Adding and Subtracting

Topics that you'll learn in this chapter:

- ✓ Adding Two–Digit Numbers

- ✓ Subtracting Two–Digit Numbers

- ✓ Adding Three–Digit Numbers

- ✓ Adding Hundreds

- ✓ Adding 4–Digit Numbers

- ✓ Subtracting 4–Digit Numbers

Adding Two–Digit Numbers

✍ Find each sum.

1) $\begin{array}{r} 84 \\ +\ 12 \\ \hline \end{array}$

2) $\begin{array}{r} 23 \\ +\ 18 \\ \hline \end{array}$

3) $\begin{array}{r} 64 \\ +\ 24 \\ \hline \end{array}$

4) $\begin{array}{r} 19 \\ +\ 19 \\ \hline \end{array}$

5) $\begin{array}{r} 66 \\ +\ 34 \\ \hline \end{array}$

6) $\begin{array}{r} 41 \\ +\ 26 \\ \hline \end{array}$

7) $\begin{array}{r} 74 \\ +\ 8 \\ \hline \end{array}$

8) $\begin{array}{r} 49 \\ +\ 37 \\ \hline \end{array}$

9) $\begin{array}{r} 70 \\ +\ 20 \\ \hline \end{array}$

10) $\begin{array}{r} 81 \\ +\ 12 \\ \hline \end{array}$

11) $\begin{array}{r} 69 \\ +\ 11 \\ \hline \end{array}$

12) $\begin{array}{r} 89 \\ +\ 35 \\ \hline \end{array}$

13) $\begin{array}{r} 91 \\ +\ 13 \\ \hline \end{array}$

14) $\begin{array}{r} 77 \\ +\ 33 \\ \hline \end{array}$

Subtracting Two–Digit Numbers

✎ Find each difference.

1) $\begin{array}{r} 19 \\ -\ 8 \\ \hline \end{array}$

2) $\begin{array}{r} 25 \\ -\ 16 \\ \hline \end{array}$

3) $\begin{array}{r} 32 \\ -\ 19 \\ \hline \end{array}$

4) $\begin{array}{r} 25 \\ -\ 25 \\ \hline \end{array}$

5) $\begin{array}{r} 58 \\ -\ 23 \\ \hline \end{array}$

6) $\begin{array}{r} 60 \\ -\ 10 \\ \hline \end{array}$

7) $\begin{array}{r} 71 \\ -\ 48 \\ \hline \end{array}$

8) $\begin{array}{r} 65 \\ -\ 31 \\ \hline \end{array}$

9) $\begin{array}{r} 72 \\ -\ 41 \\ \hline \end{array}$

10) $\begin{array}{r} 96 \\ -\ 66 \\ \hline \end{array}$

11) $\begin{array}{r} 99 \\ -\ 84 \\ \hline \end{array}$

12) $\begin{array}{r} 73 \\ -\ 43 \\ \hline \end{array}$

13) $\begin{array}{r} 51 \\ -\ 27 \\ \hline \end{array}$

14) $\begin{array}{r} 82 \\ -\ 12 \\ \hline \end{array}$

Adding Three–Digit Numbers

✎Find each sum.

1)
$$\begin{array}{r} 411 \\ + \ 26 \\ \hline \end{array}$$

8)
$$\begin{array}{r} 593 \\ + 648 \\ \hline \end{array}$$

2)
$$\begin{array}{r} 653 \\ + 241 \\ \hline \end{array}$$

9)
$$\begin{array}{r} 895 \\ + \ 134 \\ \hline \end{array}$$

3)
$$\begin{array}{r} 741 \\ + 357 \\ \hline \end{array}$$

10)
$$\begin{array}{r} 479 \\ + 139 \\ \hline \end{array}$$

4)
$$\begin{array}{r} 678 \\ + 222 \\ \hline \end{array}$$

11)
$$\begin{array}{r} 795 \\ + 343 \\ \hline \end{array}$$

5)
$$\begin{array}{r} 129 \\ + 111 \\ \hline \end{array}$$

12)
$$\begin{array}{r} 918 \\ + 527 \\ \hline \end{array}$$

6)
$$\begin{array}{r} 498 \\ + 220 \\ \hline \end{array}$$

13)
$$\begin{array}{r} 897 \\ + 365 \\ \hline \end{array}$$

7)
$$\begin{array}{r} 637 \\ + \ 120 \\ \hline \end{array}$$

14)
$$\begin{array}{r} 911 \\ + 199 \\ \hline \end{array}$$

Adding Hundreds

✎ Add.

1) $200 + 300 =$ —

2) $200 + 500 =$ —

3) $700 + 700 =$ —

4) $600 + 400 =$ —

5) $300 + 800 =$ —

6) $600 + 600 =$ —

7) $800 + 900 =$ —

8) $900 + 700 =$ —

9) $500 + 800 =$ —

10) $200 + 700 =$ —

11) $900 + 900 =$ —

12) $600 + 900 =$ —

13) $100 + 500 =$ —

14) $200 + 800 =$ —

15) If there are 900 balls in a box and Jackson puts 700 more balls inside, how many balls are in the box?

_____ balls

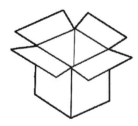

Adding 4–Digit Numbers

✎Add.

1)
$$\begin{array}{r} 2,426 \\ + 5,394 \\ \hline \end{array}$$

3)
$$\begin{array}{r} 2,530 \\ + 1,363 \\ \hline \end{array}$$

5)
$$\begin{array}{r} 8,864 \\ + 1,256 \\ \hline \end{array}$$

2)
$$\begin{array}{r} 6,256 \\ + 2,893 \\ \hline \end{array}$$

4)
$$\begin{array}{r} 7,150 \\ + 2,673 \\ \hline \end{array}$$

6)
$$\begin{array}{r} 7,231 \\ + 2,493 \\ \hline \end{array}$$

✎Find the missing numbers.

7) $1,998 + \underline{\quad} = 3,451$

10) $748 + \underline{\quad} = 2,950$

8) $700 + 3,000 = \underline{\quad}$

11) $\underline{\quad} + 956 = 3,783$

9) $2,500 + \underline{\quad} = 3,880$

12) $\underline{\quad} + 2,071 = 5,900$

13) David sells gems. He finds a diamond in Istanbul and buys it for $5,892. Then, he flies to Cairo and purchases a bigger diamond for the bargain price of $8,471. How much does David spend on the two diamonds?

Subtracting 4-Digit Numbers

✎Subtract.

1) $\begin{array}{r} 7,343 \\ -\ 4,279 \\ \hline \end{array}$

4) $\begin{array}{r} 3,534 \\ -\ 1,956 \\ \hline \end{array}$

7) $\begin{array}{r} 2,369 \\ -\ 1,233 \\ \hline \end{array}$

2) $\begin{array}{r} 8,765 \\ -\ 4,453 \\ \hline \end{array}$

5) $\begin{array}{r} 9,142 \\ -\ 5,639 \\ \hline \end{array}$

8) $\begin{array}{r} 8,450 \\ -\ 6,169 \\ \hline \end{array}$

3) $\begin{array}{r} 6,475 \\ -\ 4,954 \\ \hline \end{array}$

6) $\begin{array}{r} 7,813 \\ -5,099 \\ \hline \end{array}$

9) $\begin{array}{r} 6,000 \\ -3,223 \\ \hline \end{array}$

✎Find the missing number.

10) $5,632 -$ ___ $= 2,953$

13) $6,700 -$ ___ $= 4,968$

11) $4,572 -$ ___ $= 3,132$

14) $3,752 - 2,542 =$ ___

12) $9,231 - 5,678 =$ ___

15) $4,887 - 3,762 =$ ___

16) Jackson had \$6,973 invested in the stock market until he lost \$2,784 on those investments. How much money does he have in the stock market now?

Answers of Worksheets – Chapter 2

Adding two–digit numbers

1) 96	6) 67	11) 80
2) 41	7) 82	12) 124
3) 88	8) 86	13) 104
4) 38	9) 90	14) 110
5) 100	10) 93	

Subtracting two–digit numbers

1) 11	6) 50	11) 15
2) 9	7) 23	12) 30
3) 13	8) 34	13) 24
4) 0	9) 31	14) 70
5) 35	10) 30	

Adding three–digit numbers

1) 437	6) 718	11) 1,138
2) 894	7) 757	12) 1,445
3) 1,098	8) 1,241	13) 1,262
4) 900	9) 1,029	14) 1,110
5) 240	10) 618	

Adding hundreds

1) 500	5) 1,100	9) 1,300	13) 600
2) 700	6) 1,200	10) 900	14) 1,000
3) 1,400	7) 1,700	11) 1,800	15) 1,600
4) 1,000	8) 1,600	12) 1,500	

Adding 4–digit numbers

1) 7,820	6) 9,724	11) 2,827
2) 9,149	7) 1,453	12) 3,829
3) 3,893	8) 3,700	13) $14,363
4) 9,823	9) 1,380	
5) 10,120	10) 2,202	

Subtracting 4–digit numbers

1) 3,064

2) 4,312

3) 1,521

4) 1,578

5) 3,503

6) 2,714

7) 1,136

8) 2,281

9) 2,777

10) 2,679

11) 1,440

12) 3,553

13) 1,732

14) 1,210

15) 1,125

16) 4,189

Chapter 3:

Multiplication and Division

Topics that you'll learn in this chapter:

- ✓ Multiplication by 0, 1, 2, and 3

- ✓ Multiplication by 4, 5, 6

- ✓ Multiplication by 7, 8, 9

- ✓ Multiplication by 10, 11, 12

- ✓ Division by 0, 1, 2, 3

- ✓ Division by 4, 5, 6

- ✓ Division by 7, 8, 9

- ✓ Division by 10, 11, 12

- ✓ Dividing by Tens

- ✓ Divide 3–Digit Numbers by 1-Digit Numbers

- ✓ Multiply 1digit by 3–Digit Numbers

Multiplication by 0, 1, 2, and 3

✎Write the answers.

1) $7 \times 3 =$ ___

2) $10 \times 2 =$ ___

3) $15 \times 1 =$ ___

4) $19 \times 0 =$ ___

5) $12 \times 3 =$ ___

6) $6 \times 3 =$ ___

7) $20 \times 2 =$ ___

8) $23 \times 1 =$ ___

9) $25 \times 2 =$ ___

10) $20 \times 3 =$ ___

✎Find Each Missing Number.

11) $2 \times$ ___ $= 14$

12) $3 \times$ ___ $= 12$

13) $9 \times 2 =$ ___

14) ___ $\times 1 = 10$

15) ___ $\times 4 = 20$

16) $17 \times$ ___ $= 0$

17) $3 \times$ ___ $= 9$

18) $5 \times$ ___ $= 25$

19) $3 \times$ ___ $= 24$

20) ___ $\times 11 = 0$

21) ___ $\times 3 = 15$

22) $18 \times 0 =$ ___

23) $7 \times$ ___ $= 49$

24) ___ $\times 6 = 30$

Multiplication by 4, 5, 6

✏ Write the answers.

1) $8 \times 4 =$ __

2) $10 \times 6 =$ __

3) $9 \times 5 =$ __

4) $3 \times 6 =$ __

5) $8 \times 6 =$ __

6) $4 \times 4 =$ __

7) $9 \times 4 =$ __

8) $7 \times 5 =$ __

9) $10 \times 4 =$ __

10) $10 \times 6 =$ __

11) $12 \times 5 =$ __

12) $11 \times 6 =$ __

13) $20 \times 4 =$ __

14) $15 \times 4 =$ __

15) $30 \times 5 =$ __

16) $16 \times 5 =$ __

17) Ryan ordered ten pizzas and sliced them into nine pieces each. How many pieces of pizza were there?

_____

Multiplication by 7, 8, 9

✎ Write the answers.

1) $6 \times 7 =$ ___

2) $10 \times 8 =$ ___

3) $5 \times 9 =$ ___

4) $5 \times 7 =$ ___

5) $10 \times 7 =$ ___

6) $20 \times 7 =$ ___

7) $12 \times 8 =$ ___

8) $9 \times 9 =$ ___

9) $11 \times 7 =$ ___

10) $10 \times 8 =$ ___

11) $15 \times 7 =$ ___

12) $20 \times 8 =$ ___

13) $30 \times 7 =$ ___

14) $13 \times 7 =$ ___

15) $16 \times 8 =$ ___

16) $17 \times 7 =$ ___

17) There are 6 bananas in each box. How many bananas are in 8 boxes? _____

18) Each child has 10 apples. If there are 7 children, how many apples are there in

total? _____

Multiplication by 10, 11, 12

✎Write the answers.

1) 6 × 10 = __

2) 3 × 11 = __

3) 5 × 12 = __

4) 8 × 11 = __

5) 10 × 11 = __

6) 7 × 12 = __

7) 6 × 11 = __

8) 2 × 12 = __

9) 4 × 12 = __

10) 11 × 11 = __

11) 5 × 10 = __

12) 7 × 11 = __

13) 13 × 10 = __

14) 9 × 11 = __

15) 20 × 10 = __

16) 30 × 11 = _

17) 5 × 11 = _

18) 16 × 10 = _

19) 20 × 11 = _

20) 15 × 12 = _

21) Each child has 6 pencils. If there are 11 children, how many pens are there in total?

_____ pencils

Division by 0, 1, 2, 3

Find each missing number.

1) $66 \div \underline{} = 33$

2) $22 \div 2 = \underline{}$

3) $15 \div 3 = \underline{}$

4) $50 \div 2 = \underline{}$

5) $\underline{} \div 3 = 7$

6) $18 \div 3 = \underline{}$

7) $\underline{} \div 2 = 10$

8) $40 \div \underline{} = 20$

9) $\underline{} \div 3 = 11$

10) $\underline{} \div 2 = 18$

11) $\underline{} \div 3 = 2$

12) $3 \div 3 = \underline{}$

13) $28 \div \underline{} = 14$

14) $16 \div 2 = \underline{}$

15) $8 \div \underline{} = 4$

16) $\underline{} \div 3 = 9$

17) $\underline{} \div 3 = 10$

18) $22 \div \underline{} = 22$

19) $30 \div 2 = \underline{}$

20) $\underline{} \div 3 = 0$

21) Jessica has 33 strawberries that she would like to give to her 3 friends. If she shares them equally, how many strawberries will she give to each of her friends?

_____ strawberries

Division by 4, 5, 6

✎ Find each missing number.

1) $50 \div 5 = \underline{\quad}$

2) $40 \div \underline{\quad} = 8$

3) $60 \div \underline{\quad} = 10$

4) $35 \div \underline{\quad} = 7$

5) $24 \div 4 = \underline{\quad}$

6) $60 \div 4 = \underline{\quad}$

7) $\underline{\quad} \div 4 = 5$

8) $66 \div \underline{\quad} = 11$

9) $80 \div 4 = \underline{\quad}$

10) $6 \div \underline{\quad} = 1$

11) $65 \div \underline{\quad} = 13$

12) $12 \div \underline{\quad} = 2$

13) $42 \div \underline{\quad} = 7$

14) $\underline{\quad} \div 4 = 10$

15) $48 \div 6 = \underline{\quad}$

16) $18 \div 6 = \underline{\quad}$

17) $\underline{\quad} \div 4 = 10$

18) $55 \div 5 = \underline{\quad}$

19) $72 \div 6 = \underline{\quad}$

20) $\underline{\quad} \div 4 = 15$

21) Hanna has 70 marbles that she would like to give to her 5 friends. If she shares them equally, how many marbles will she give to each?

_____ marbles

Division by 7, 8, 9

✎Find each missing number.

1) __ ÷ 9 = 1

2) __ ÷ 8 = 3

3) 88 ÷ 8 = __

4) 32 ÷ __ = 4

5) 27 ÷ 9 = __

6) __ ÷ 8 = 12

7) 91 ÷ __ = 13

8) __ ÷ 7 = 15

9) 54 ÷ __ = 6

10) 16 ÷ 8 = __

11) __ ÷ 7 = 12

12) 21 ÷ __ = 3

13) __ ÷ 7 = 18

14) 80 ÷ 8 = __

15) 64 ÷ __ = 8

16) 81 ÷ 9 = __

17) 99 ÷ 9 = __

18) 63 ÷ 9 = __

19) 70 ÷ 7 = __

20) 77 ÷ 7 = __

21) Emily has 91 fruit juice that she would like to give to her 7 friends. If she shares them equally, how many fruit juices will she give to each?

_____ fruit juice

Division by 10, 11, 12

Find each missing number.

1) $10 \div \_\_ = 1$

2) $121 \div 11 = \_\_$

3) $99 \div \_\_ = 9$

4) $30 \div 10 = \_\_$

5) $12 \div \_\_ = 1$

6) $40 \div \_\_ = 4$

7) $\_\_ \div 12 = 6$

8) $144 \div 12 = \_\_$

9) $110 \div \_\_ = 10$

10) $90 \div \_\_ = 9$

11) $\_\_ \div 12 = 7$

12) $\_\_ \div 12 = 11$

13) $70 \div \_\_ = 7$

14) $\_\_ \div 12 = 5$

15) $84 \div 12 = \_\_$

16) $80 \div 10 = \_\_$

17) $96 \div 12 = \_\_$

18) $120 \div \_\_ = 12$

19) $143 \div 11 = \_\_$

20) $220 \div \_\_ = 20$

21) Anna has 120 books. She wants to put them in equal numbers on 12 bookshelves. How many books can she put on a bookshelf? _____ books

22) If dividend is 110 and the quotient is 11, then what is the divisor? _____

Dividing by Tens

✎Find answers.

1) $600 \div 20 =$

2) $900 \div 90 =$

3) $800 \div 40 =$

4) $770 \div 10 =$

5) $180 \div 20 =$

6) $990 \div 90 =$

7) $630 \div 70 =$

8) $810 \div 90 =$

9) $420 \div 60 =$

10) $640 \div 40 =$

11) $300 \div 50 =$

12) $180 \div 60 =$

13) $800 \div 50 =$

14) $270 \div 90 =$

15) $400 \div 40 =$

16) $120 \div 40 =$

17) $200 \div 10 =$

18) $930 \div 30 =$

19) $\dfrac{360}{20}$

20) $\dfrac{900}{30}$

21) $\dfrac{700}{70}$

22) $\dfrac{450}{90}$

23) $\dfrac{210}{30}$

24) $\dfrac{420}{60}$

Divide 3–Digit Numbers by 1-Digit Numbers

✎Find the answers.

1) $750 \div 6 = $ ____

2) $360 \div 9 = $ ____

3) $480 \div 3 = $ ____

4) $1,085 \div 7 = $ ____

5) $480 \div 8 = $ ____

6) $180 \div 9 = $ ____

7) $800 \div 4 = $ ____

8) $700 \div 7 = $ ____

9) $250 \div 5 = $ ____

10) $420 \div 6 = $ ____

11) $400 \div 8 = $ ____

12) $320 \div 4 = $ ____

13) $240 \div 6 = $ ____

14) $630 \div 9 = $ ____

15) $360 \div 6 = $ ____

16) $550 \div 2 = $ ____

17) $420 \div 6 = $ ____

18) $720 \div 5 = $ ____

19) $720 \div 3 = $ ____

20) $450 \div 5 = $ ____

21) $660 \div 6 = $ ____

22) $930 \div 3 = $ ____

Multiply 1digit by 3–Digit Numbers

✎ Find the answers.

1)
$$\begin{array}{r} 530 \\ \times\ 6 \\ \hline \end{array}$$

9)
$$\begin{array}{r} 195 \\ \times\ 6 \\ \hline \end{array}$$

2)
$$\begin{array}{r} 260 \\ \times\ 4 \\ \hline \end{array}$$

10)
$$\begin{array}{r} 911 \\ \times\ 3 \\ \hline \end{array}$$

3)
$$\begin{array}{r} 470 \\ \times\ 4 \\ \hline \end{array}$$

11)
$$\begin{array}{r} 657 \\ \times\ 5 \\ \hline \end{array}$$

4)
$$\begin{array}{r} 340 \\ \times\ 8 \\ \hline \end{array}$$

12)
$$\begin{array}{r} 258 \\ \times\ 3 \\ \hline \end{array}$$

5)
$$\begin{array}{r} 940 \\ \times\ 2 \\ \hline \end{array}$$

13)
$$\begin{array}{r} 325 \\ \times\ 8 \\ \hline \end{array}$$

6)
$$\begin{array}{r} 432 \\ \times\ 5 \\ \hline \end{array}$$

14)
$$\begin{array}{r} 125 \\ \times\ 6 \\ \hline \end{array}$$

7)
$$\begin{array}{r} 365 \\ \times\ 6 \\ \hline \end{array}$$

15)
$$\begin{array}{r} 213 \\ \times\ 7 \\ \hline \end{array}$$

8)
$$\begin{array}{r} 255 \\ \times\ 8 \\ \hline \end{array}$$

16)
$$\begin{array}{r} 444 \\ \times\ 6 \\ \hline \end{array}$$

Times Table

×	1	2	3	4	5	6	7	8	9	10	11	12
1	1	2	3	4	5	6	7	8	9	10	11	12
2	2	4	6	8	10	12	14	16	18	20	22	24
3	3	6	9	12	15	18	21	24	27	30	33	36
4	4	8	12	16	20	24	28	32	36	40	44	48
5	5	10	15	20	25	30	35	40	45	50	55	60
6	6	12	18	24	30	36	42	48	54	60	66	72
7	7	14	21	28	35	42	49	56	63	70	77	84
8	8	16	24	32	40	48	56	64	72	80	88	96
9	9	18	27	36	45	54	63	72	81	90	99	108
10	10	20	30	40	50	60	70	80	90	100	110	120
11	11	22	33	44	55	66	77	88	99	110	121	132
12	12	24	36	48	60	72	84	96	108	120	132	144

Answers of Worksheets – Chapter 3

Multiplication by 0, 1, 2, 3

1) 21
2) 20
3) 15
4) 0
5) 36
6) 18
7) 40
8) 23

9) 50
10) 60
11) 7
12) 4
13) 18
14) 10
15) 5
16) 0

17) 3
18) 5
19) 8
20) 0
21) 5
22) 0
23) 7
24) 5

Multiplication by 4, 5, 6

1) 32
2) 60
3) 45
4) 18
5) 48
6) 16

7) 36
8) 35
9) 40
10) 60
11) 60
12) 66

13) 80
14) 60
15) 150
16) 80
17) 90

Multiplication by 7, 8, 9

1) 42
2) 80
3) 45
4) 35
5) 70
6) 140

7) 96
8) 81
9) 77
10) 80
11) 105
12) 160

13) 210
14) 91
15) 128
16) 119
17) 48
18) 70

Multiplication by 10, 11, 12

1) 60
2) 33
3) 60
4) 88
5) 110
6) 84

7) 66
8) 24
9) 48
10) 121
11) 50
12) 77

13) 130
14) 99
15) 200
16) 330
17) 55
18) 160

19) 220   20) 180   21) 66

Division by 0, 1, 2, 3

1) 2   8) 2   15) 2
2) 11   9) 33   16) 27
3) 5   10) 36   17) 30
4) 25   11) 6   18) 1
5) 21   12) 1   19) 15
6) 6   13) 2   20) 0
7) 20   14) 8   21) 11

Division by 4, 5, 6

1) 10   8) 6   15) 8
2) 5   9) 20   16) 3
3) 6   10) 6   17) 40
4) 5   11) 5   18) 11
5) 6   12) 6   19) 12
6) 15   13) 6   20) 60
7) 20   14) 40   21) 14

Division by 7, 8, 9

1) 9   8) 105   15) 8
2) 24   9) 9   16) 9
3) 11   10) 2   17) 11
4) 8   11) 84   18) 7
5) 3   12) 7   19) 10
6) 96   13) 126   20) 11
7) 7   14) 10   21) 13

Division by 10, 11, 12

1) 10   6) 10   11) 84
2) 11   7) 60   12) 132
3) 11   8) 12   13) 10
4) 3   9) 11   14) 60
5) 12   10) 10   15) 7

16) 3

17) 8

18) 10

19) 13

20) 11

21) 10

22) 10

Dividing by tens

1) 30

2) 10

3) 20

4) 77

5) 9

6) 11

7) 9

8) 9

9) 7

10) 8

11) 6

12) 3

13) 16

14) 3

15) 10

16) 3

17) 20

18) 31

19) 18

20) 30

21) 10

22) 5

23) 7

24) 7

Divide 3-digit numbers by 1-digit numbers

1) 125

2) 40

3) 160

4) 155

5) 60

6) 20

7) 200

8) 100

9) 50

10) 70

11) 50

12) 80

13) 40

14) 70

15) 60

16) 275

17) 70

18) 144

19) 240

20) 90

21) 110

22) 310

Multiply 1digit by 3 digits

1) 3,180

2) 1,040

3) 1,880

4) 2,720

5) 1,880

6) 2,160

7) 2,190

8) 2,040

9) 1,170

10) 2,733

11) 3,285

12) 774

13) 2,600

14) 750

15) 1,491

16) 2,664

Chapter 4: Spatial sense, Estimation and rounding

Topics that you'll learn in this chapter:

- ✓ Rounding Numbers

- ✓ Estimate Sums

- ✓ Estimate Differences

- ✓ Estimate Products

- ✓ Missing Numbers

Rounding Numbers

✎ Round each number to the underlined place value.

1) 4,8<u>6</u>4	11) 8,6<u>1</u>7	21) <u>8</u>,348
2) 2,<u>9</u>61	12) <u>8</u>,380	22) 9,7<u>5</u>4
3) 1,2<u>8</u>6	13) 5,7<u>5</u>6	23) 9,<u>8</u>47
4) 7,5<u>7</u>3	14) 6,<u>5</u>19	24) 6,<u>6</u>93
5) 4,7<u>5</u>6	15) 3,<u>8</u>64	25) 3,9<u>6</u>2
6) 6,5<u>3</u>6	16) 6,<u>5</u>72	26) 9,<u>8</u>91
7) 1,6<u>8</u>3	17) 6,5<u>8</u>2	27) <u>5</u>,975
8) 4,9<u>8</u>7	18) 7,6<u>2</u>7	28) 3,5<u>7</u>4
9) 6,<u>6</u>78	19) 9,4<u>5</u>6	29) 7,4<u>3</u>6
10) 2,4<u>2</u>4	20) 3,<u>7</u>15	30) 8,<u>8</u>94

Estimate Sums

✎ Estimate the sum by rounding each added to the nearest ten.

1) $64 + 9$

2) $25 + 55$

3) $83 + 6$

4) $26 + 52$

5) $44 + 54$

6) $36 + 16$

7) $61 + 45$

8) $26 + 35$

9) $46 + 40$

10) $24 + 36$

11) $49 + 16$

12) $64 + 24$

13) $81 + 7$

14) $42 + 56$

15) $96 + 39$

16) $72 + 82$

17) $79 + 46$

18) $66 + 76$

19) $75 + 28$

20) $56 + 49$

21) $93 + 82$

22) $58 + 46$

23) $48 + 92$

24) $57 + 47$

25) $28 + 56$

26) $41 + 91$

27) $65 + 69$

Estimate Differences

Estimate the difference by rounding each number to the nearest ten.

1) $46 - 14 =$

2) $35 - 16 =$

3) $58 - 34 =$

4) $65 - 17 =$

5) $45 - 26 =$

6) $57 - 29 =$

7) $97 - 85 =$

8) $46 - 10 =$

9) $73 - 46 =$

10) $81 - 45 =$

11) $56 - 34 =$

12) $80 - 6 =$

13) $95 - 46 =$

14) $36 - 12 =$

15) $80 - 50 =$

16) $76 - 42 =$

17) $57 - 24 =$

18) $38 - 19 =$

19) $55 - 24 =$

20) $68 - 32 =$

21) $86 - 42 =$

22) $57 - 51 =$

23) $69 - 52 =$

24) $93 - 54 =$

25) $37 - 12 =$

26) $86 - 43 =$

27) $98 - 55 =$

Estimate Products

✏️ Estimate the products.

1) 24 × 12	11) 56 × 24	21) 82 × 65
2) 26 × 11	12) 61 × 22	22) 84 × 32
3) 28 × 13	13) 57 × 33	23) 51 × 43
4) 45 × 17	14) 68 × 23	24) 61 × 73
5) 37 × 21	15) 59 × 29	25) 84 × 53
6) 44 × 82	16) 64 × 42	26) 72 × 25
7) 34 × 45	17) 69 × 43	27) 48 × 39
8) 48 × 27	18) 62 × 20	28) 92 × 11
9) 35 × 24	19) 71 × 26	29) 47 × 13
10) 66 × 11	20) 83 × 45	30) 59 × 44

Missing Numbers

✎ Find the missing numbers.

1) $40 \times \underline{} = 80$

2) $18 \times \underline{} = 72$

3) $\underline{} \times 17 = 68$

4) $15 \times \underline{} = 105$

5) $\underline{} \times 21 = 63$

6) $16 \times \underline{} = 32$

7) $\underline{} \times 1 = 50$

8) $32 \times \underline{} = 128$

9) $20 \times \underline{} = 80$

10) $19 \times 6 = \underline{}$

11) $14 \times 7 = \underline{}$

12) $43 \times 4 = \underline{}$

13) $12 \times 8 = \underline{}$

14) $\underline{} \times 25 = 150$

15) $44 \times \underline{} = 220$

16) $36 \times 5 = \underline{}$

17) $10 \times \underline{} = 80$

18) $15 \times \underline{} = 135$

19) $\underline{} \times 13 = 91$

20) $23 \times 8 = \underline{}$

21) $\underline{} \times 21 = 189$

22) $18 \times \underline{} = 90$

23) $16 \times 8 = \underline{}$

24) $21 \times 10 = \underline{}$

25) $\underline{} \times 28 = 112$

26) $25 \times \underline{} = 175$

Answers of Worksheets – Chapter 4

Rounding Numbers

1) 4,900	11) 8,620	21) 8,000
2) 3,000	12) 8,000	22) 9,750
3) 1,290	13) 5,760	23) 9,800
4) 7,570	14) 6,500	24) 6,700
5) 4,760	15) 3,900	25) 3,960
6) 6,540	16) 6,600	26) 9,900
7) 1,680	17) 6,580	27) 6,000
8) 4,990	18) 7,630	28) 3,570
9) 6,700	19) 9,460	29) 7,440
10) 2,420	20) 3,700	30) 8,900

Estimate sums

1) 70	10) 60	19) 110
2) 90	11) 70	20) 110
3) 90	12) 80	21) 170
4) 80	13) 90	22) 110
5) 90	14) 100	23) 140
6) 60	15) 140	24) 110
7) 110	16) 150	25) 90
8) 70	17) 130	26) 130
9) 90	18) 150	27) 140

Estimate differences

1) 40	9) 20	17) 40
2) 20	10) 30	18) 20
3) 30	11) 30	19) 40
4) 50	12) 70	20) 40
5) 20	13) 50	21) 50
6) 30	14) 30	22) 10
7) 10	15) 30	23) 20
8) 40	16) 40	24) 40

25) 30   26) 50   27) 40

Estimate products

1) 288	11) 1,344	21) 5,330
2) 286	12) 1,342	22) 2,688
3) 364	13) 1,881	23) 2,193
4) 765	14) 1,564	24) 4,453
5) 777	15) 1,711	25) 4,452
6) 3,608	16) 2,688	26) 1,800
7) 1,530	17) 2,967	27) 1,872
8) 1,296	18) 1,240	28) 1,012
9) 840	19) 1,846	29) 611
10) 726	20) 3,735	30) 2,596

Missing Numbers

1) 2	10) 114	19) 7
2) 4	11) 98	20) 184
3) 4	12) 172	21) 9
4) 7	13) 96	22) 5
5) 3	14) 6	23) 128
6) 2	15) 5	24) 210
7) 50	16) 180	25) 4
8) 4	17) 8	26) 7
9) 4	18) 9	

Chapter 5: Fractions

Topics that you'll learn in this chapter:

- ✓ Fractions

- ✓ Fractions of a Number

- ✓ Order Fractions

- ✓ Simplifying Fractions

- ✓ Improper Fraction

- ✓ Comparing Fractions

- ✓ Missing Denominator or Numerator

Fractions

Color $\frac{1}{4}$ of each shape.

$$\frac{1}{4} = \frac{2}{8}$$

1)

2)

$$\frac{1}{4} = \frac{3}{12}$$

3)

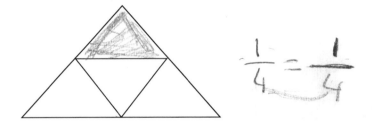

$$\frac{1}{4} = \frac{1}{4}$$

Shade the lower parts to make the fractions equivalent, then write the fractions.

4)

$$\frac{2}{6}$$

$$\frac{2}{6} = \frac{1}{3}$$

Fractions of a Number

✎ Solve.

1) Find $\frac{1}{2}$ of 80

2) Find $\frac{1}{2}$ of 50

3) Find $\frac{1}{2}$ of 90

4) Find $\frac{3}{4}$ of 40

5) Find $\frac{1}{5}$ of 30

6) Find $\frac{3}{7}$ of 49

7) Find $\frac{1}{6}$ of 48

8) Find $\frac{2}{9}$ of 27

9) Find $\frac{1}{9}$ of 72

10) Find $\frac{5}{7}$ of 35

11) Find $\frac{3}{8}$ of 24

12) Find $\frac{2}{3}$ of 45

13) Find $\frac{1}{10}$ of 110

14) Find $\frac{1}{8}$ of 56

15) Find $\frac{3}{14}$ of 140

16) Find $\frac{5}{9}$ of 81

17) Find $\frac{5}{7}$ of 770

18) Find $\frac{5}{7}$ of 63

19) Find $\frac{3}{4}$ of 16

20) Find $\frac{5}{18}$ of 180

Order Fractions

✎ Order the fractions from greatest to latest.

1) $\frac{1}{9}, \frac{5}{3}, \frac{2}{3}$

2) $\frac{2}{5}, \frac{3}{8}, \frac{7}{6}$

3) $\frac{2}{7}, \frac{8}{9}, \frac{1}{12}$

4) $\frac{13}{5}, \frac{3}{4}, \frac{14}{11}$

5) $\frac{5}{7}, \frac{5}{4}, \frac{3}{8}$

6) $\frac{1}{10}, \frac{6}{7}, \frac{3}{5}$

7) $\frac{9}{7}, \frac{1}{5}, \frac{3}{4}$

8) $\frac{11}{7}, \frac{3}{5}, \frac{5}{8}$

9) $\frac{4}{9}, \frac{1}{7}, \frac{2}{5}$

10) $\frac{8}{5}, \frac{1}{6}, \frac{5}{6}$

✎ Order the fractions from latest to greatest.

11) $\frac{1}{5}, \frac{2}{7}, \frac{1}{3}$

12) $\frac{1}{5}, \frac{3}{8}, \frac{1}{6}$

13) $\frac{3}{7}, \frac{5}{9}, \frac{1}{10}$

14) $\frac{3}{5}, \frac{3}{4}, \frac{4}{9}$

15) $\frac{1}{2}, \frac{3}{4}, \frac{3}{10}$

16) $\frac{1}{8}, \frac{1}{4}, \frac{3}{7}$

17) $\frac{4}{7}, \frac{3}{5}, \frac{1}{3}$

18) $\frac{11}{9}, \frac{3}{5}, \frac{5}{6}$

Simplifying Fractions

✏️Simplify the following fractions.

1) $\frac{7}{21} =$

2) $\frac{6}{42} =$

3) $\frac{20}{80} =$

4) $\frac{13}{39} =$

13) $\frac{5}{30} =$

14) $\frac{5}{40} =$

15) $\frac{63}{72} =$

16) $\frac{25}{50} =$

5) $\frac{8}{24} =$

6) $\frac{8}{64} =$

7) $\frac{10}{20} =$

8) $\frac{4}{36} =$

17) $\frac{30}{24} =$

18) $\frac{11}{66} =$

19) $\frac{48}{54} =$

20) $\frac{36}{63} =$

9) $\frac{5}{50} =$

10) $\frac{11}{33} =$

11) $\frac{7}{28} =$

12) $\frac{18}{42} =$

21) $\frac{52}{65} =$

22) $\frac{15}{60} =$

23) $\frac{25}{30} =$

24) $\frac{32}{64} =$

Improper Fraction

🖎 Fill in the blank.

1) $\frac{1}{2} + \underline{} = 2$

2) $\frac{1}{3} + \underline{} = 3$

3) $\frac{1}{4} + \underline{} = 1$

4) $\frac{5}{7} + \underline{} = 1$

5) $\frac{9}{4} + \underline{} = 4$

6) $\frac{2}{3} + \underline{} = 4$

7) $\frac{4}{5} + \underline{} = 3$

8) $\frac{1}{6} + \underline{} = 3$

9) $\frac{7}{3} + \underline{} = 5$

10) $\frac{1}{2} + \underline{} = 5$

11) $\frac{17}{9} + \underline{} = 2$

12) $\frac{5}{2} + \underline{} = 3$

13) $\frac{5}{2} + \underline{} = 6$

14) $\frac{13}{6} + \underline{} = 3$

15) $\frac{17}{3} + \underline{} = 7$

16) $\frac{9}{2} + \underline{} = 7$

17) $\frac{5}{4} + \underline{} = 3$

18) $\frac{7}{8} + \underline{} = 2$

19) $\frac{23}{4} + \underline{} = 7$

20) $\frac{5}{4} + \underline{} = 5$

Comparing Fractions

✐ Use > = < to compare fractions.

1) $\frac{1}{2} \boxed{>} \frac{3}{6}$

2) $\frac{5}{20} \boxed{<} \frac{1}{2}$

3) $\frac{13}{26} \square \frac{4}{16}$

4) $\frac{4}{6} \square \frac{2}{3}$

5) $\frac{10}{60} \square \frac{1}{6}$

6) $\frac{18}{30} \square \frac{7}{8}$

7) $\frac{5}{25} \square \frac{10}{50}$

8) $\frac{24}{12} \square \frac{10}{12}$

9) $\frac{1}{7} \square \frac{1}{7}$

10) $\frac{12}{48} \square \frac{1}{4}$

Missing Denominator or Numerator

✐ Find the missing values.

1) $\frac{1}{5} = \frac{}{25}$

2) $\frac{}{6} = \frac{8}{12}$

3) $\frac{}{10} = \frac{1}{5}$

4) $\frac{8}{24} = \frac{1}{}$

5) $\frac{}{48} = \frac{7}{56}$

6) $\frac{8}{40} = \frac{}{5}$

7) $\frac{4}{28} = \frac{1}{}$

8) $\frac{6}{25} = \frac{12}{}$

9) $\frac{8}{72} = \frac{}{9}$

10) $\frac{2}{28} = \frac{}{14}$

Answers of Worksheets – Chapter 5

Fractions

1)

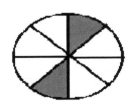

2)

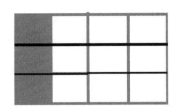

3)

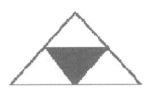

4) $\frac{2}{6} = \frac{1}{3}$

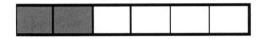

Fractions of a number

1) 40	8) 6	15) 30
2) 25	9) 8	16) 45
3) 45	10) 25	17) 550
4) 30	11) 9	18) 45
5) 6	12) 30	19) 12
6) 21	13) 11	20) 50
7) 8	14) 7	

Order fractions

1) $\frac{5}{3}, \frac{2}{3}, \frac{1}{9}$

2) $\frac{7}{6}, \frac{2}{5}, \frac{3}{8}$

3) $\frac{8}{9}, \frac{2}{7}, \frac{1}{12}$

4) $\frac{13}{5}, \frac{14}{11}, \frac{3}{4}$

5) $\frac{5}{4}, \frac{5}{7}, \frac{3}{8}$

6) $\frac{6}{7}, \frac{3}{5}, \frac{1}{10}$

7) $\frac{9}{7}, \frac{3}{4}, \frac{1}{5}$

8) $\frac{11}{7}, \frac{5}{8}, \frac{3}{5}$

9) $\frac{4}{9}, \frac{2}{5}, \frac{1}{7}$

10) $\frac{8}{5}, \frac{5}{6}, \frac{1}{6}$

11) $\frac{1}{5}, \frac{2}{7}, \frac{1}{3}$

12) $\frac{1}{6}, \frac{1}{5}, \frac{3}{8}$

13) $\frac{1}{10}, \frac{3}{7}, \frac{5}{9}$

14) $\frac{4}{9}, \frac{3}{5}, \frac{3}{4}$

15) $\frac{3}{10}, \frac{1}{2}, \frac{3}{4}$

16) $\frac{1}{8}, \frac{1}{4}, \frac{3}{7}$

17) $\frac{1}{3}, \frac{4}{7}, \frac{3}{5}$

18) $\frac{3}{5}, \frac{5}{6}, \frac{11}{9}$

Simplifying Fractions

1) $\frac{1}{3}$

2) $\frac{1}{7}$

3) $\frac{1}{4}$

4) $\frac{1}{3}$

5) $\frac{1}{3}$ 10) $\frac{1}{3}$ 15) $\frac{7}{8}$ 20) $\frac{4}{7}$

6) $\frac{1}{8}$ 11) $\frac{1}{4}$ 16) $\frac{1}{2}$ 21) $\frac{4}{5}$

7) $\frac{1}{2}$ 12) $\frac{3}{7}$ 17) $\frac{5}{4}$ 22) $\frac{1}{4}$

8) $\frac{1}{9}$ 13) $\frac{1}{6}$ 18) $\frac{1}{6}$ 23)

9) $\frac{1}{10}$ 14) $\frac{1}{8}$ 19) $\frac{8}{9}$ 24) $\frac{1}{2}$

Improper Fraction

1) $\frac{3}{2}$ 6) $\frac{10}{3}$ 11) $\frac{1}{9}$ 16) $\frac{5}{2}$

2) $\frac{8}{3}$ 7) $\frac{11}{5}$ 12) $\frac{1}{2}$ 17) $\frac{7}{4}$

3) $\frac{3}{4}$ 8) $\frac{17}{6}$ 13) $\frac{7}{2}$ 18) $\frac{9}{8}$

4) $\frac{2}{7}$ 9) $\frac{8}{3}$ 14) $\frac{5}{6}$ 19) $\frac{5}{4}$

5) $\frac{7}{4}$ 10) $\frac{9}{2}$ 15) $\frac{4}{3}$ 20) $\frac{15}{4}$

Comparing fractions

1) $\frac{1}{2} = \frac{3}{6}$ 6) $\frac{18}{30} < \frac{7}{8}$

2) $\frac{5}{20} < \frac{1}{2}$ 7) $\frac{5}{25} = \frac{10}{50}$

3) $\frac{13}{26} > \frac{4}{16}$ 8) $\frac{24}{12} > \frac{10}{12}$

4) $\frac{4}{6} = \frac{2}{3}$ 9) $\frac{1}{7} = \frac{1}{7}$

5) $\frac{10}{60} = \frac{1}{6}$ 10) $= \frac{1}{4}$

Find the missing values

1) 5   4) 3   7) 7   10) 1

2) 4   5) 6   8) 50

3) 2   6) 1   9) 1

Chapter 6: Time and Money

Topics that you'll learn in this chapter:

- ✓ Read Clocks

- ✓ Telling Time

- ✓ Electronic Clock

- ✓ Measurement – Time

- ✓ Calendars

- ✓ Add Money Amounts

- ✓ Subtract Money Amounts

- ✓ Money: Word Problems

Read Clocks

✍ Write the time below each clock.

1)

_____

2)

_____

3)

_____

4)

_____

5)

_____

6)

_____

Telling Time

1) What time is shown by this clock?

_____

2) It is night. What time is shown on this clock?

_____

✎ Draw the hands on the clock face.

3)

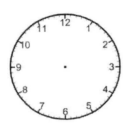

......05:10.......

4)

......09:25.......

5)

......06:50.......

6)

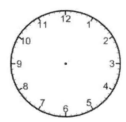

......07:55.......

Digital Clock

What time is it? Write the time in words in front of each.

1) 5: 45 _____

2) 6: 30 _____

3) 9: 15 _____

4) 7: 25 _____

5) 3: 35 _____

6) 11: 05 _____

7) 4: 15 _____

8) 2: 20 _____

Measurement – Time

How much time has passed?

1) 2:25 AM to 6:45 AM: _____ hours and _____ minutes.

2) 1:10 AM to 6:15 AM: _____ hours and _____ minutes.

3) 5:00 AM. to 6:15 AM. = _____ hour(s) and _____ minutes.

4) 7:10 PM to 9:25 PM. = _____ hour(s) and _____ minutes

5) 8:15 A.M. to 8:45 A.M. = _____ minutes

6) 6:25 A.M. to 6:50 A.M. = _____ minutes

7) There are _____ second in 15 minutes.

8) There are _____ second in 17 minutes.

9) There are _____ second in 22 minutes.

10) There are _____ minutes in 30 hours.

11) There are _____ minutes in 8 hours.

12) There are _____ minutes in 11 hours

13) There are _____ minutes in 35 hours

14) There are _____ minutes in 13 hours.

Calendars

February						
Sun	Mon	Tue	Wed	Thu	Fri	Sat
			1	2	3	4
5	6	7	8	9	10	11
12	13	14	15	16	17	18
19	20	21	22	23	24	25
26	27	28	.			

1. How many Friday are in the calendar?

   _____

2. What is the day on the 6th of February?

   _____

3. What is the date in the second Sunday of the month?

   _____

Money Amounts

✎ Add.

1)
$$\begin{array}{r} \$458 \\ +\$184 \\ \hline \end{array}$$
$$\begin{array}{r} \$654 \\ +\$280 \\ \hline \end{array}$$
$$\begin{array}{r} \$586 \\ +\$315 \\ \hline \end{array}$$

2)
$$\begin{array}{r} \$357 \\ +\$378 \\ \hline \end{array}$$
$$\begin{array}{r} \$615 \\ +\$299 \\ \hline \end{array}$$
$$\begin{array}{r} \$645 \\ +\$214 \\ \hline \end{array}$$

3)
$$\begin{array}{r} \$575 \\ +\$298 \\ \hline \end{array}$$
$$\begin{array}{r} \$741 \\ +\$280 \\ \hline \end{array}$$
$$\begin{array}{r} \$758 \\ +\$288 \\ \hline \end{array}$$

4)
$$\begin{array}{r} \$925 \\ +\$215 \\ \hline \end{array}$$
$$\begin{array}{r} \$610 \\ +\$112 \\ \hline \end{array}$$
$$\begin{array}{r} \$780 \\ +\$420 \\ \hline \end{array}$$

✎ Subtract.

1)
$$\begin{array}{r} \$845 \\ -\$259 \\ \hline \end{array}$$
$$\begin{array}{r} \$815 \\ -\$198 \\ \hline \end{array}$$
$$\begin{array}{r} \$548 \\ -\$218 \\ \hline \end{array}$$

2)
$$\begin{array}{r} \$685 \\ -\$325 \\ \hline \end{array}$$
$$\begin{array}{r} \$559 \\ -\$259 \\ \hline \end{array}$$
$$\begin{array}{r} \$869 \\ -\$750 \\ \hline \end{array}$$

3)
$$\begin{array}{r} \$390 \\ -\$121 \\ \hline \end{array}$$
$$\begin{array}{r} \$645 \\ -\$254 \\ \hline \end{array}$$
$$\begin{array}{r} \$785 \\ -\$625 \\ \hline \end{array}$$

4) Linda had $17.70. She bought some game tickets for $8.10. How much did she have left?

Money: Word Problems

Solve.

1) How many boxes of envelopes can you buy with $30 if one box costs $6?

2) After paying $6.35 for a salad, Ella has $50.36. How much money did she have before buying the salad?

3) How many packages of diapers can you buy with $90 if one package costs $9?

4) Last week James ran 42 miles more than Michael. James ran 87 miles. How many miles did Michael run?

5) Last Friday Jacob had $27.83. Over the weekend he received some money for cleaning the attic. He now has $68. How much money did he receive?

6) After paying $14.17 for a sandwich, Amelia has $29.52. How much money did she have before buying the sandwich?

Answers of Worksheets – Chapter 6

Read clocks

1) 4: 00

2) 10: 30

3) 7: 15

4) 1: 35

5) 5: 45

6) 8: 15

Telling Time

1) 7:50

2) 6:00

3)

4)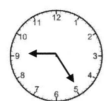

5)

6)

Digital Clock

1) It's five forty–five.

2) It's six thirty.

3) It's nine Fifteen.

4) It's seven twenty- five.

5) It's three thirty-five.

6) It's eleven five.

7) It's four Fifteen.

8) It's two twenty.

Measurement – Time

1) 4:20

2) 5:05

3) 1:15

4) 2:15

5) 30 minutes

6) 25 minutes

7) 900

8) 1,020

9) 1,320

10) 1,800

11) 480

12) 660

13) 2,100

14) 780

Calendars

1) 4

2) Monday

3) 12th

Add Money Amounts

1) 642; 934; 901

2) 735; 914; 859

3) 873; 1,021; 1,046

4) 1,140; 722; 1,200

Subtract Money Amounts

1) 586; 617; 330

2) 360; 300; 119

3) 269; 391; 160

4) 9.60

Money: word problem

1) 5

2) $56.71

3) 10

4) 45

5) 40.17

6) 15.35

Chapter 7: Measurement

Topics that you'll learn in this chapter:

- ✓ Reference Measurement

- ✓ Metric Length

- ✓ Customary Length

- ✓ Metric Capacity

- ✓ Customary Capacity

- ✓ Metric Weight and Mass

- ✓ Customary Weight and Mass

Reference Measurement

LENGTH

Customary	Metric
1 mile (mi) = 1,760 yards (yd)	1 kilometer (km) = 1,000 meters (m)
1 yard (yd) = 3 feet (ft)	1 meter (m) = 100 centimeters (cm)
1 foot (ft) = 12 inches (in.)	1 centimeter(cm)= 10 millimeters(mm)

VOLUME AND CAPACITY

Customary	Metric
1 gallon (gal) = 4 quarts (qt)	1 liter (L) = 1,000 milliliters (mL)
1 quart (qt) = 2 pints (pt.)	
1 pint (pt.) = 2 cups (c)	
1 cup (c) = 8 fluid ounces (Fl oz)	

WEIGHT AND MASS

Customary	Metric
1 ton (T) = 2,000 pounds (lb.)	1 kilogram (kg) = 1,000 grams (g)
1 pound (lb.) = 16 ounces (oz)	1 gram (g) = 1,000 milligrams (mg)

Time

1 year = 12 months

1 year = 52 weeks

1 week = 7 days

1 day = 24 hours

1 hour = 60 minutes

1 minute = 60 seconds

Metric Length Measurement

✎ Convert to the units.

1) 200 mm = _____ cm

2) 4 m = _____ mm

3) 5 m = _____ cm

4) 6 km = _____ m

5) 8,000mm = _____ m

6) 900 cm = _____ m

7) 11 m = _____ cm

8) 2,000 mm = _____ cm

9) 4,000 mm = _____ m

10) 6 km = _____ mm

11) 12 km = _____ m

12) 40 m = _____ cm

13) 8,000 m = _____ km

14) 9,000 m = _____ km

Customary Length Measurement

✎ Convert to the units.

1) 6 ft = _____ in

2) 3 ft = _____ in

3) 3 yd = _____ ft

4) 5 yd = _____ ft

5) 3 yd = _____ in

6) 36 in = _____ ft

7) 252 in = _____ yd

8) 180in = _____ yd

9) 20yd = _____ in

10) 58yd = _____ in

11) 81ft = _____ yd

12) 150ft = _____ yd

13) 96in = _____ ft

14) 60 yd = _____ feet

Metric Capacity Measurement

✎Convert the following measurements.

1) 40 l = _____ ml

2) 6 l = _____ ml

3) 40 l = _____ ml

4) 32 l = _____ ml

5) 27 l = _____ ml

6) 13 l = _____ ml

7) 80,000 l = _____ l

8) 56,000 mml = _____ l

9) 95,000 ml = _____ l

10) 4,000 ml = _____ l

11) 10,000 ml = _____ l

12) 70, 000 ml = _____ l

Customary Capacity Measurement

✎Convert the following measurements.

1) 78 gal = _____ qt.

2) 44 gal = _____ pt.

3) 75 gal = _____ c.

4) 15 pt. = _____ c

5) 18 qt = _____ pt.

6) 19 qt = _____ c

7) 28 pt. = _____ c

8) 64 c = _____ gal

9) 128 pt. = _____ gal

10) 112 qt = _____ gal

11) 164 pt. = _____ qt

12) 88 c = _____ qt

13) 156 c = _____ pt.

14) 192 qt = _____ gal

15) 130 pt. = _____ qt

16) 86 gal = _____ pt.

Metric Weight and Mass Measurement

✍Convert.

1) 40 kg = _____ g

2) 45 kg = _____ g

3) 500 kg = _____ g

4) 50 kg = _____ g

5) 55 kg = _____ g

6) 80 kg = _____ g

7) 78 kg = _____ g

8) 62,000 g = _____ kg

9) 530,000 g = _____ kg

10) 400,000 g = _____ kg

11) 30,000 g = _____ kg

12) 20,000 g = _____ kg

13) 850,000 g = _____ kg

14) 900,000 g = _____ kg

Customary Weight and Mass Measurement

✍Convert.

1) 6,000 lb. = _____ T

2) 12,000 lb. = _____ T

3) 8,000 lb. = _____ T

4) 14,000lb. = _____ T

5) 32 lb. = _____ oz

6) 46lb.=_____ oz

7) 135lb. = _____ oz

8) 2T =_____ lb.

9) 9T = _____ lb.

10) 12T =_____ lb.

11) 15T =_____ lb.

12) 8T = _____ oz

13) 6T = _____ oz

14) 13T=_____ oz

Answers of Worksheets – Chapter 7

Metric length

1) 20 cm	6) 9 m	11) 12,000 m
2) 4,000 mm	7) 1,100 cm	12) 4,000 cm
3) 500 cm	8) 20 cm	13) 8 km
4) 6,000 m	9) 4 m	14) 9 km
5) 8 m	10) 6,000,000 mm	

Customary Length

1) 72	6) 3	11) 27
2) 36	7) 7	12) 50
3) 9	8) 5	13) 8
4) 15	9) 720	14) 180
5) 108	10) 2,088	

Metric Capacity

1) 40,000 ml	5) 27,000 ml	9) 95 ml
2) 6,000 ml	6) 13,000 ml	10) 4L
3) 40,000 ml	7) 80 ml	11) 10 L
4) 32,000 ml	8) 56 ml	12) 70 L

Customary Capacity

1) 312 qt	5) 36 pt.	9) 16 gal	13) 78 pt.
2) 352 pt.	6) 76c	10) 28 gal	14) 48 gal
3) 1,200 c	7) 56 c	11) 82 qt	15) 65 qt
4) 30 c	8) 8 gal	12) 22qt	16) 688 pt.

Metric Weight and Mass

1) 40,000 g	6) 80,000 g	11) 30 kg
2) 45,000 g	7) 78,000 g	12) 20 kg
3) 500,000 g	8) 62 kg	13) 850 kg
4) 50,000 g	9) 530 kg	14) 900 kg
5) 55,000 g	10) 400 kg	

Customary Weight and Mass

1) 3 T

2) 6 T

3) 4 T

4) 7 T

5) 512 oz

6) 736 oz

7) 2,160 oz

8) 4,000 lb.

9) 18,000 lb.

10) 24,000 lb.

11) 30,000 lb.

12) 256,000 oz

13) 192,000 oz

14) 416,000 oz

Chapter 8: Symmetry and Transformations

Topics that you'll learn in this chapter:

- ✓ Line Segments

- ✓ Identify Lines of Symmetry

- ✓ Count Lines of Symmetry

- ✓ Parallel, Perpendicular and Intersecting Lines

- ✓ Translations, Rotations, and Reflections

Line Segments

✍ Write each as a line, ray or line segment.

1)

2)

3)

4)

5)

6)

7)

8)

Identify Lines of Symmetry

✎ Tell whether the line on each shape a line of symmetry is.

1)

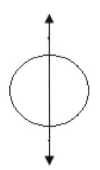

2)

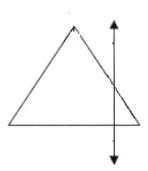

3)

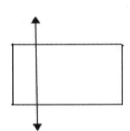

4)

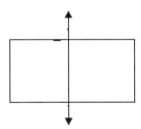

5)

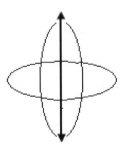

6)

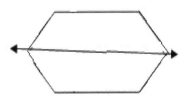

7)

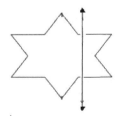

8)

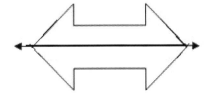

Count Lines of Symmetry

Draw lines of symmetry on each shape. Count and write the lines of symmetry you see.

1)

2)

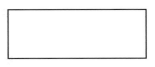

3)

4)

5)

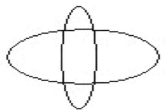

6)

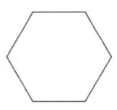

7)

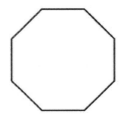

8)

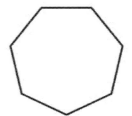

Parallel, Perpendicular and Intersecting Lines

State whether the given pair of lines are parallel, perpendicular, or intersecting.

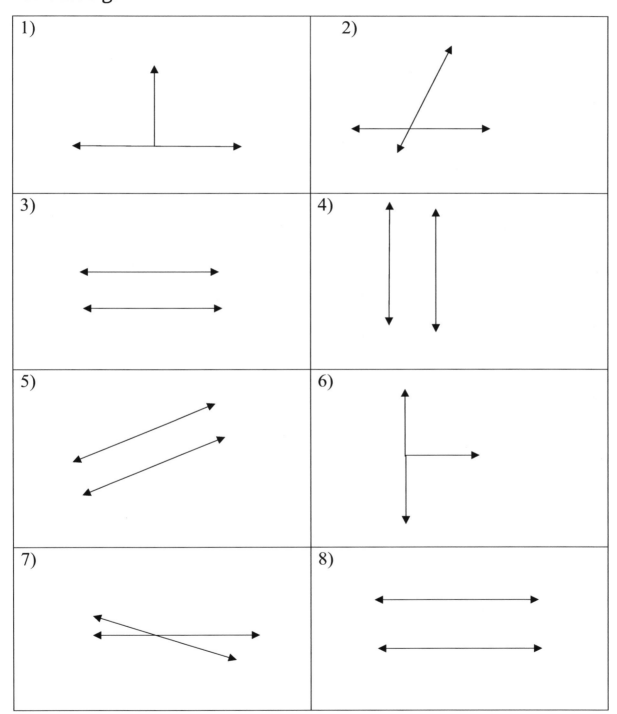

Answers of Worksheets – Chapter 8

Line Segments

1) Line segment

2) Ray

3) Line

4) Line segment

5) Ray

6) Line

7) Line

8) Line segment

Identify lines of symmetry

1) yes

2) no

3) no

4) yes

5) yes

6) yes

7) no

8) yes

Count lines of symmetry

1)

2)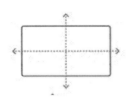

3)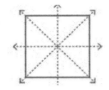

4)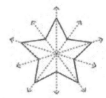

5)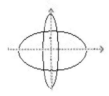

6)

7)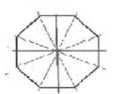

8)

Parallel, Perpendicular and Intersecting Lines

1) Perpendicular

2) Intersection

3) Parallel

4) Parallel

5) Parallel

6) Perpendicular

7) Intersection

8) Parallel

Chapter 9: Geometric

Topics that you'll learn in this chapter:

- ✓ Identifying Angles: Acute, Right, Obtuse, and Straight Angles

- ✓ Polygon Names

- ✓ Classify Triangles

- ✓ Parallel Sides in Quadrilaterals

- ✓ Identify Parallelograms

- ✓ Identify Trapezoids

- ✓ Identify Rectangles

- ✓ Perimeter and Area of Squares

- ✓ Perimeter and Area of rectangles

- ✓ Area and Perimeter: Word Problems

Identifying Angles

✎ Write the name of the angles (Acute, Right, Obtuse, and Straight).

1)

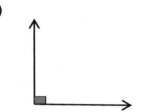

2)

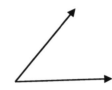

3)

4)

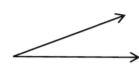

5)

6)

7)

8)

Polygon Names

✎ Write name of polygons.

1)

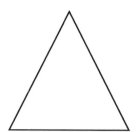

2)

3)

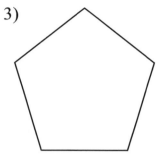

4)

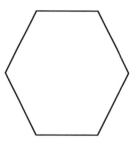

5)

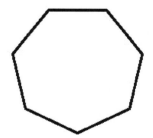

6)

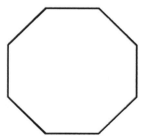

Classify Triangles

Classify the triangles by their sides and angles.

1)

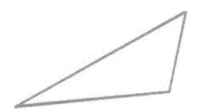

2)

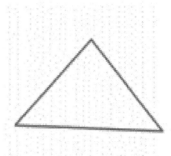

3)

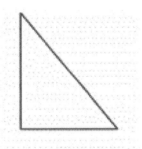

4)

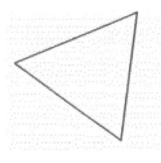

5)

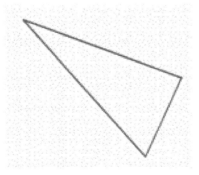

6)

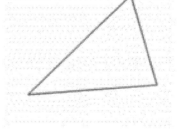

Parallel Sides in Quadrilaterals

Write name of quadrilaterals.

1)

2)

3)

4)

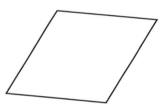

5)

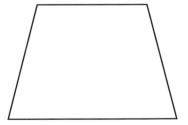

6)

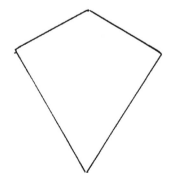

Identify Rectangles

✎ Solve.

1) A rectangle has _____ sides and _____ angles.

2) Draw a rectangle that is 7centimeters long and 3 centimeters wide. What is the perimeter?

3) Draw a rectangle 4 cm long and 2 cm wide.

4) Draw a rectangle whose length is 5 cm and whose width is 3 cm. What is the perimeter of the rectangle?

5) What is the perimeter of the rectangle?

6

8

Perimeter: Find the Missing Side Lengths

✎ Find the missing side of each shape.

1) perimeter = 80

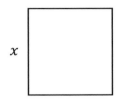

2) perimeter = 28

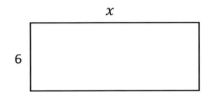

3) perimeter = 60

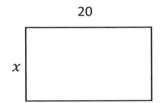

4) perimeter = 20

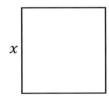

5) perimeter = 60

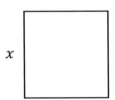

6) perimeter = 26

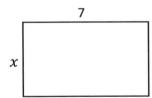

7) perimeter = 52

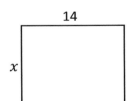

8) perimeter = 24

Perimeter and Area of Squares

Find perimeter and area of squares.

1) A: _____, P: _____

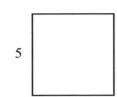
5

2) A: _____, P: _____

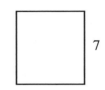
7

3) A: _____, P: _____

8

4) A: _____, P: _____

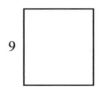
9

5) A: _____, P: _____

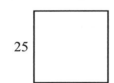
25

6) A: _____, P: _____

13

7) A: _____, P: _____

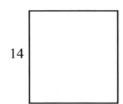
14

8) A: _____, P: _____

15

Perimeter and Area of rectangles

 Find perimeter and area of rectangles.

1) A: _____ , P: _____

8

4

2) A: _____ , P: _____

4

3

3) A: _____ , P: _____

4

6

4) A: _____ , P: _____

12

10

5) A: _____ , P: _____

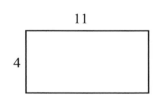

11

4

6) A: _____ , P: _____

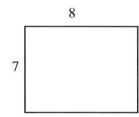

8

7

7) A: _____ , P: _____

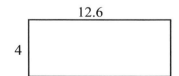

12.6

4

8) A: _____ , P: _____

14.6

8

Find the Area or Missing Side Length of a Rectangle

✎ Find area or missing side length of rectangles.

1) Area =?

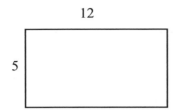

2) Area = 42, x=?

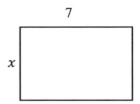

3) Area = 54, x=?

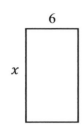

4) Area =?

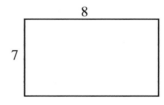

5) Area =?

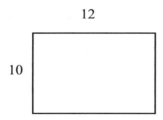

6) Area = 500, x=?

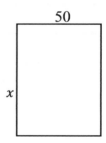

7) Area = 650, x=?

8) Area 624, x=?

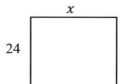

Area and Perimeter: Word Problems

✎ Solve.

1) The area of a rectangle is 96 square meters. The width is 8 meters. What is the

   length of the rectangle?

2) A square has an area of 64 square feet. What is the perimeter of the square?

3) Ava built a rectangular vegetable garden that is 5 feet long and has an area of

   45 square feet. What is the perimeter of Ava's vegetable garden?

4) A square has a perimeter of 96 millimeters. What is the area of the square?

5) The perimeter of David's square backyard is 88 meters. What is the area of

   David's backyard?

6) The area of a rectangle is 32 square inches. The length is 8 inches. What is the

   perimeter of the rectangle?

Answers of Worksheets – Chapter 9

Identifying Angles

1) Obtuse
2) Acute

3) Right
4) Acute

5) Straight
6) Obtuse

7) Obtuse
8) Acute

Polygon Names

1) Triangle
2) Quadrilateral

3) Pentagon
4) Hexagon

5) Heptagon
6) Octagon

Classify triangles

1) Scalene, obtuse
2) Isosceles, right

3) Scalene, right
4) Equilateral, acute

5) Isosceles, acute
6) Scalene, acute

Parallel Sides in Quadrilaterals

1) Square
2) Rectangle

3) Parallelogram
4) Rhombus

5) Trapezoid
6) Kike

Identify Rectangles

1) 4 - 4
2) 20

3) Draw the square
4) 16

5) 28

Perimeter: Find the Missing Side Lengths

1) 20
2) 8

3) 10
4) 5

5) 15
6) 6

7) 12
8) 6

Perimeter and Area of Squares

1) A: 25, P: 20
2) A: 49, P: 28
3) A: 64, P: 32

4) A: 81, P: 36
5) A: 625 P: 100
6) A: 169, P: 52

7) A: 196, P: 56
8) A: 225, P: 60

Perimeter and Area of rectangles

1) A: 32, P: 24
2) A: 12, P: 14
3) A: 24, P: 20

4) A: 120, P: 44
5) A: 44, P: 30
6) A: 56, P: 30

7) A: 50.4, P: 33.2
8) A: 116.8, P: 45.2

Find the Area or Missing Side Length of a Rectangle

1) 60
2) 6

3) 9
4) 56

5) 120
6) 10

7) 26
8) 26

Area and Perimeter: Word Problems

1) 12
2) 32

3) 28
4) 576

5) 484
6) 24

Chapter 10: Data and Graphs

Topics that you'll learn in this chapter:

✓ Graph Points on a Coordinate Plane

✓ Bar Graph

✓ Tally and Pictographs

✓ Line Graphs

Graph Points on a Coordinate Plane

Plot each point on the coordinate grid.

1) A (5, 8)   3) C (2, 6)   5) E (1, 7)

2) B (4, 5)   4) D (7, 6)   6) F (8, 1)

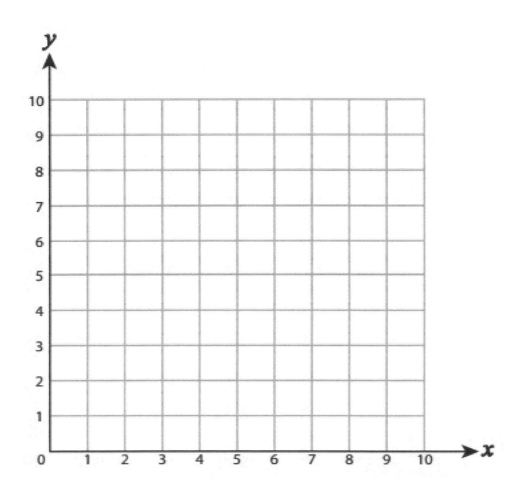

Bar Graph

✎ Graph the given information as a bar graph.

Day	Hot dogs sold
Monday	40
Tuesday	70
Wednesday	20
Thursday	90
Friday	60

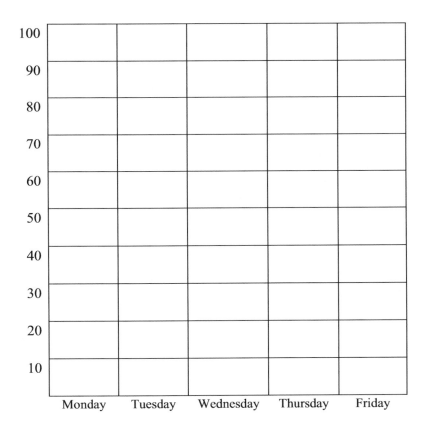

Tally and Pictographs

Using the key, draw the pictograph to show the information.

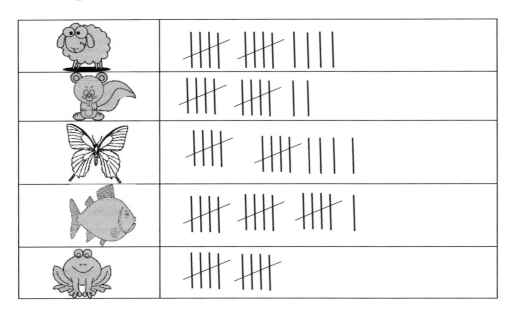

Key: ⚽ = 2 animals

Line Graphs

David work as a salesman in a store. He records the number of shoes sold in five days on a line graph. Use the graph to answer the question.

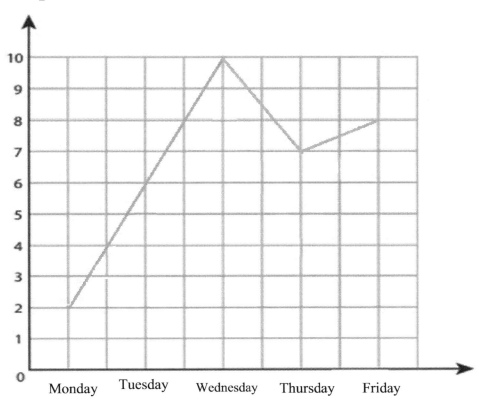

1) How many shoes were sold on Tuesday?

2) Which day had the minimum sales of shoes?

3) Which day had the maximum number of shoes sold?

4) How many shoes were sold in 5 days?

Answers of Worksheets – Chapter 10

Graph Points on a Coordinate Plane

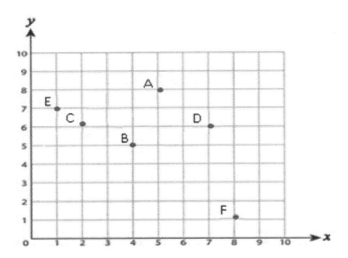

Bar Graph

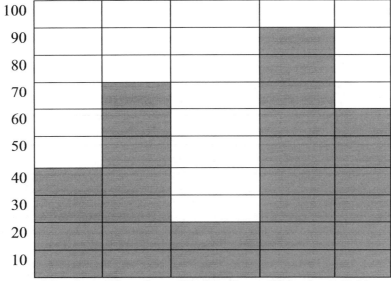

Tally and Pictographs

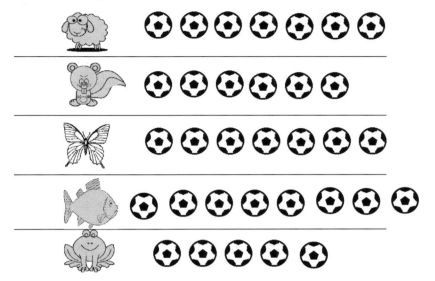

Line Graphs

1) 6   2) Monday   3) Wednesday   4) 33

PSSA Math Practice Tests

Time to Test

Time to refine your skill with a practice examination

Take a REAL PSSA Mathematics test to simulate the test day experience. After you've finished, score your test using the answer key.

Before You Start

- You'll need a pencil and scratch papers to take the test.

- For this practice test, don't time yourself. Spend time as much as you need.

- It's okay to guess. You won't lose any points if you're wrong.

- After you've finished the test, review the answer key to see where you went wrong.

Calculators are not permitted for Grade 3 PSSA Tests

Good Luck!

PSSA GRADE 3 MAHEMATICS REFRENCE MATERIALS

LENGTH

Customary	Metric
1 mile (mi) = 1,760 yards (yd)	1 kilometer (km) = 1,000 meters (m)
1 yard (yd) = 3 feet (ft)	1 meter (m) = 100 centimeters (cm)
1 foot (ft) = 12 inches (in.)	1 centimeter (cm) = 10 millimeters (mm)

VOLUME AND CAPACITY

Customary	Metric
1 gallon (gal) = 4 quarts (qt)	1 liter (L) = 1,000 milliliters (mL)
1 quart (qt) = 2 pints (pt.)	
1 pint (pt.) = 2 cups (c)	
1 cup (c) = 8 fluid ounces (Fl oz)	

WEIGHT AND MASS

Customary	Metric
1 ton (T) = 2,000 pounds (lb.)	1 kilogram (kg) = 1,000 grams (g)
1 pound (lb.) = 16 ounces (oz)	1 gram (g) = 1,000 milligrams (mg)

Time

1 year = 12 months

1 year = 52 weeks

1 week = 7 days

1 day = 24 hours

1 hour = 60 minutes

1 minute = 60 seconds

The Pennsylvania System of School Assessment

PSSA Practice Test 1

Mathematics

GRADE 3

- ❖ **20 questions**
- ❖ **Calculators are not permitted for this practice test**

Pennsylvania Department of Education Bureau of Curriculum, Assessment

and Instruction— *Month Year*

1) There are 3 days in a weekend. There are 24 hours in day. How many hours are in a weekend?

   A. 72

   B. 48

   C. 68

   D. 200

2) This clock shows a time after 2:15 PM. What time was it 2 hours and 30 minutes ago?

   A. 12:15 PM

   B. 11:45 PM

   C. 12: 15 AM

   D. 11:45 AM

3) A football team is buying new uniforms. Each uniform cost $20. The team wants to buy 14 uniforms.

   Which equation represents a way to find the total cost of the uniforms?

   A. $(20 \times 10) + (1 \times 14) = 200 + 14$

   B. $(20 \times 10) + (10 \times 4) = 200 + 40$

   C. $(20 \times 10) + (20 \times 4) = 200 + 80$

   D. $(14 \times 10) + (10 \times 20) = 140 + 200$

4) Olivia has 168 pastilles. She wants to put them in boxes of 4 pastilles. How many boxes does she need?

    A. 38

    B. 42

    C. 34

    D. 48

5) Mia's goal is to save $148 to purchase her favorite bike.

    - In January, she saved $54.

    - In February, she saved $29.

How much money does Mia need to save in March to be able to purchase her favorite bike?

    A. $83

    B. $38

    C. $56

    D. $65

6) Michelle has 96 old books. She plans to send all of them to the library in their area. If she puts the books in boxes which can hold 6 books, which of the following equations can be used to find the number of boxes she will use?

    A. $96 + 6 =$ _____

    B. $96 \times 6 =$ _____

    C. $96 - 6 =$ _____

    D. $96 \div 6 =$ _____

7) Elise had 864 cards. Then, she gave 286 of the cards to her friend Alice. After that, Elise lost 195 cards.

Which equation can be used to find the number of cards Elise has now?

A. $864 - 286 + 195 =$ _____

B. $864 - 286 - 195 =$ _____

C. $864 + 286 + 195 =$ _____

D. $864 + 286 - 195 =$ _____

8) The length of the following rectangle is 12 centimeters and its width is 6 centimeters. What is the area of the rectangle?

A. 60 cm^2

B. 24 cm^2

C. 72 cm^2

D. 36 cm^2

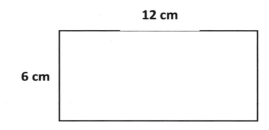

9) Look at the spinner above. On which color is the spinner most likely to land?

A. Red

B. Green

C. Yellow

D. None

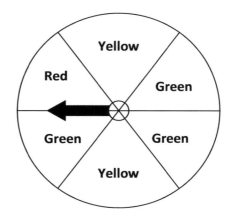

10) A group of third grade students recorded the following distances that they jumped.

21 inches	38 inches	24 inches	29 inches
35 inches	33 inches	38 inches	34 inches
31 inches	29 inches	34 inches	38 inches

What is the distance that was jumped most often?

A. 21

B. 29

C. 34

D. 38

11) Emma flew 4,451 miles from Los Angeles to New York City. What is the number of miles Emma flew rounded to the nearest thousand?

A. 5,000

B. 4,400

C. 4,500

D. 4,000

12) To what number is the arrow pointing?

A. 12

B. 14

C. 18

D. 10

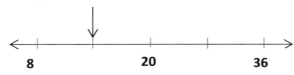

13) A number sentence such as $36 + Z = 81$ can be called an equation. If this equation is true, then which of the following equations is not true?

A. $81 - 36 = Z$

B. $81 - Z = 36$

C. $Z - 81 = 36$

D. $Z = 45$

14) Which number correctly completes the number sentence $60 \times 48 =$?

A. 350

B. 700

C. 1,350

D. 2,880

15) Which of the following statements describes the number 34,976?

A. The sum of three thousands, 4 thousands, nine hundreds, seventy tens, and six ones

B. The sum of forty thousands, 3 thousands, nine hundreds, seven tens, and six ones

C. The sum of thirty thousands, 4 thousands, ninety hundreds, seventy tens, and six ones

D. The sum of thirty thousands, 4 thousands, nine hundreds, seven tens, and six ones

16) Use the models below to answer the question.

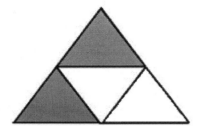 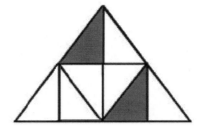

Which statement about the models is true?

A. Each shows the same fraction because they are the same size.

B. Each shows a different fraction because they are different shapes.

C. Each shows the same fraction because they both have 2 sections shaded.

D. Each shows a different fraction because they both have 2 shaded sections but

a different number of total sections.

17) Classroom A contains 9 rows of chairs with 6 chairs per row. If classroom B has

two times as many chairs, which number sentence can be used to find the number

of chairs in classroom B?

A. $9 \times 6 + 2$

B. $9 + 6 \times 2$

C. $9 \times 6 \times 2$

D. $9 + 6 + 2$

18) Which number correctly completes the subtraction sentence

$6,000 - 965 = $ _____?

A. 5,035

B. 5,350

C. 350

D. 5,305

19) Jason packs 16 boxes with flashcards. Each box holds 45 flashcards. How many flashcards Jason can pack into these boxes?

A. 270

B. 860

C. 680

D. 720

20) A cafeteria menu had spaghetti with meatballs for $10 and bean soup for $5 How much would it cost to buy four plates of spaghetti with meatballs and four bowls of bean soup?

Write your answer in the box below.

_____

"This is the end of the practice test 1"

The Pennsylvania System of School Assessment

PSSA Practice Test 2

Mathematics

GRADE 3

❖ **20 questions**

❖ **Calculators are not permitted for this practice test**

Pennsylvania Department of Education Bureau of Curriculum, Assessment

and Instruction— *Month Year*

1) Kayla has 100 red cards and 66 white cards. How many more reds cards than white cards do Kayla have?

   A. 14

   B. 10

   C. 34

   D. 24

2) A number sentence is shown below.

$6 \times 9 \,\square\, 5 = 49$

What symbol goes into the box to make the number sentence true?

   A. $\times$

   B. $\div$

   C. $+$

   D. $-$

3) Liam had 761 marbles. Then, he gave 254 of the cards to his friend Ethan. After that, Liam lost 163 cards.

Which equation can be used to find the number of cards Eve has now?

A. $761 - 754 + 163 =$ _____

B. $761 - 254 - 163 =$ _____

C. $761 + 254 + 163 =$ _____

D. $761 + 254 - 163 =$ _____

4) What is the value of "B" in the following equation?

$$51 + B + 4 = 69$$

   A. 16

   B. 18

   C. 24

   D. 14

5) There are two different cards on the table.

-    There are 5 rows that have 10 red cards in each row.

-    There are 36 white cards.

How many cards are there on the table?

   A. 65

   B. 86

   C. 36

   D. 99

6) Which of the following list shows only fractions that are equivalent to $\frac{1}{4}$?

   A. $\frac{2}{8}, \frac{3}{12}, \frac{8}{32}$

   B. $\frac{6}{24}, \frac{5}{8}, \frac{9}{32}$

   C. $\frac{3}{12}, \frac{4}{8}, \frac{6}{24}$

   D. $\frac{3}{12}, \frac{5}{15}, \frac{8}{32}$

7) What mixed number is shown by the shaded triangles?

A. $2\frac{1}{3}$

B. $3\frac{1}{4}$

C. $2\frac{1}{4}$

D. $2\frac{3}{4}$

8) Mason is 15 months now and he usually eats five meals a day. How many meals does he eat in two weeks?

A. 35

B. 80

C. 70

D. 98

9) The perimeter of a square is 20 units. Each side of this square is the same length. What is the length of one side of the square in units?

A. 4

B. 10

C. 6

D. 5

10) Which of the following comparison of fractions is true?

A. $\frac{5}{6} = \frac{32}{36}$

B. $\frac{6}{22} > \frac{3}{11}$

C. $\frac{4}{14} < \frac{5}{11}$

D. $\frac{4}{15} < \frac{4}{20}$

11) The sum of 5 ten thousand, 4 hundred, and 7 tens can be expressed as what number in standard form?

A. 5,470

B. 50,470

C. 50,047

D. 50,407

12) What is the perimeter of the following triangle?

A. 65 inches

B. 55 inches

C. 60 inches

D. 150 inches

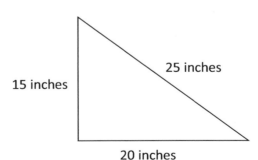

13) Moe has 360 cards. He wants to put them in boxes of 15 cards. How many boxes does he need?

    A. 20

    B. 22

    C. 23

    D. 24

14) What is the perimeter of this rectangle?

    A. 12 cm

    B. 24 cm

    C. 32 cm

    D. 64 cm

8 cm

4 cm

15) Nicole has 6 quarters, 10 dimes, and 8 pennies. How much money does Nicole have?

    A. 310 pennies

    B. 258 pennies

    C. 255 pennies

    D. 265 pennies

16) Noah packs 19 boxes with crayons. Each box holds 20 crayons. How many crayons Noah can pack into these boxes?

A. 380

B. 440

C. 580

D. 320

17) There are 60 minutes in an hour. How many minutes are in 9 hours?

A. 540 minutes

B. 520 minutes

C. 560 minutes

D. 600 minutes

18) There are 6 rows of chairs in a classroom with 9 chairs in each row. How many chairs are in the classroom?

A. 45

B. 54

C. 56

D. 63

19) Which number correctly completes the number sentence $64 \times 23 = ?$

    A. 1,572

    B. 1,740

    C. 1,472

    D. 1,750

20) Michael has 635 marbles. What is this number rounded to the nearest ten?

Write your answer in the box below.

"This is the end of practice test 2"

Answers and Explanations

PSSA Practice Tests

Answer Key

❋ Now, it's time to review your results to see where you went wrong and what areas you need to improve!

PSSA - Mathematics							
Practice Test - 1				**Practice Test - 2**			
1	A	11	D	1	C	11	B
2	D	12	B	2	D	12	C
3	C	13	C	3	B	13	D
4	B	14	D	4	D	14	B
5	D	15	D	5	B	15	B
6	D	16	D	6	A	16	A
7	B	17	C	7	B	17	A
8	C	18	A	8	C	18	B
9	B	19	D	9	D	19	C
10	D	20	60	10	C	20	640

Practice Test 1

PSSA - Mathematics

Answers and Explanations

1) Answer: A.

1 day: 24 hours

3 days = 3 × 24 = 72 hours

2) Answer: D.

The clock shows 2:15 PM. Two hour before that was 12:15 PM. 30 minutes before that was 11:45 AM.

3) Answer: C.

The Football team buys 14 uniforms that each uniform cost $20. Therefore, they should pay (14 × $20 =) $280.

Choice C is the correct answer. (20 × 10) + (20 × 4) = 200 + 80 = 280

4) Answer: B.

Olivia wants to put 168 pastilles into boxes of 4 pastilles. Therefore, she needs (168 ÷ 4 =) 42 boxes.

5) Answer: D.

Mia saved $54 and $29. Therefore, she has $83 now.

$148 - $83 = $65. She needs to save 65.

6) Answer: D.

Michelle puts 96 books in 6 boxes. Therefore, 96 ÷ 6 formula is correct.

7) Answer: B.

Elise gave 286 of her 864 cards to her friend. Therefore, she has 864 – 286 cards now. Then she lost 195 cards. Now, she has (864 – 286 – 195) = 383 cards

8) Answer: C.

Use area formula of a rectangle:

Area = length × width

Area = 12cm × 6cm = 72 cm^2

9) Answer: B.

The chance of landing on yellow is 2 out of 6.

The chance of landing on red is 1 out of 6.

The chance of landing on green is 3 out of 6.

The chance of landing on green is more than the chance of landing on other colors.

10) Answer: D.

38 is the most frequent number in the table.

11) Answer: D.

The number 4,451 rounded to the nearest thousand is 4,000.

12) Answer: B.

The arrow shows a number between two numbers 8 and 20. $(20 - 8 = 12 , 12 \div 2 = 6) \Rightarrow 8 + 6 = 14$

Therefore, the answer is 14.

13) Answer: C.

$36 + Z = 81$. Then, $Z = (81 - 36) = 45$.

All these equations are true:

$81 - 36 = Z$

$81 - Z = 36$

$Z = 45$

But this equation is not true: $Z - 81 = 36$

14) Answer: D.

$60 \times 48 = 2,880$

15) Answer: D.

34,976 is the sum of:

$30,000 + 4,000 + 900 + 70 + 6$

16) Answer: D.

The first model from left is divided into 4 equal parts. 2 out of 4 parts are shaded. The fraction for this model is $\frac{1}{2}$. The second model is divided into 8 equal parts. 2 out of 8 parts are shaded. Therefore, the fraction of the shaded parts for this model is $\frac{1}{4}$. These two models represent different fractions.

17) Answer: C.

Classroom A contains 9 rows of chairs with 6 chairs per row. Therefore, there are $(9 \times 6 =)$ 54 chairs in Classroom A. Classroom B has two times as many chairs. Then, there are $(9 \times 6 \times 2)$ chairs in Classroom B.

18) Answer: A.

$6,000 - 965 = 5,035$

19) Answer: D.

To find the answer, multiply 16 by 45.

$16 \times 45 = 720$

20) Answer: 60.

4 plates of spaghetti with meatballs cost: $4 \times \$10 = \$40$

4 bowls of bean soup cost: $4 \times \$5 = \$20$

4 plates of spaghetti with meatballs + 4 bowls of bean soup cost:

$\$40 + \$20 = \$60$

Practice Test 2

PSSA - Mathematics

Answers and Explanations

1) Answer: C.

To find the answer subtract 66 from 100. The answer is $(100 - 66) = 34$.

2) Answer: D.

$6 \times 9 = 54$. Then:

$6 \times 9 \;\square\; 5 = 49$

$54 \;\square\; 5 = 49 \Rightarrow 49 = 54 - 5$

3) Answer: B.

Liam gave 254 of his marbles to his friend. Now he has $761 - 254 = 507$

He lost 163 of his marbles. Now, he has $507 - 163 = 344$ or

$(761 - 254 - 163)$.

4) Answer: D.

$51 + B + 4 = 69 \Rightarrow 55 + B = 69 \Rightarrow B = 69 - 55 = 14$

5) Answer: B.

5 rows that have 10 red cards in each row contain: $5 \times 10 = 50$ red cards

And there are 36 white cards on table. Therefore, there are $50 + 36 = 86$ cards on

table.

6) Answer: A.

All these fractions; $\frac{2}{8}, \frac{3}{12}, \frac{8}{32}$ are equivalent to $\frac{1}{4}$.

7) Answer: B.

This shape shows 3 complete shaded triangles and 1 parts of a triangle divided

into 4 equal parts. It is equal to $3\frac{1}{4}$.

8) Answer: C.

If Mason eats 5 meals in 1 day, then, in a week (7days) he eats ($7 \times 5 = 35$) meals, in two weeks ($35 \times 2 = 70$)

9) Answer: D.

Perimeter of the square is 20. Then: $20 = 4 \times$ side $\Rightarrow$ side $= 5$

Each side of the square is 5 units.

10) Answer: C.

By comparing $\frac{4}{14}$ and $\frac{5}{11}$ we conclude that $\frac{5}{11}$ is greater than $\frac{4}{14}$. Only option C is correct.

11) Answer: B.

5 ten thousand = 50,000

4 hundred = 400

7 tens = 70

Add all: $50,000 + 400 + 70 = 50,470$

12) Answer: C.

To find the perimeter of the triangle, add all three sides.

Perimeter $= 15 + 20 + 25 = 60$ inches

13) Answer: D.

Moe wants to put 360 cards into boxes of 15 cards. Therefore, he needs ($360 \div 15 =$) 24 boxes.

14) Answer: B.

Use perimeter of rectangle formula.

Perimeter $= 2 \times$ length $+ 2 \times$ width $\Rightarrow$ P$= 2 \times 4 + 2 \times 8 = 8 + 16 = 24$ cm

15) Answer: B.

6 quarters $= 6 \times 25$ pennies $= 150$ pennies

10 dimes $= 10 \times 10$ pennies $= 100$ pennies

In total Nicole has 258 pennies

16) Answer: A.

$19 \times 20 = 380$

17) Answer: A.

1 hour = 60 minutes

9 hours = 9×60 minutes $\Rightarrow$ 9 hours = 540 minutes

18) Answer: B.

6 rows of chairs with 9 chairs in each row means: $6 \times 9 = 54$ chairs in total.

19) Answer: C.

$64 \times 23 = 1,472$

20) Answer: 640.

We round the number up to the nearest ten if the last digit in the number is 5, 6, 7, 8, or 9.

We round the number down to the nearest ten if the last digit in the number is 1, 2, 3, or 4.

If the last digit is 0, then we do not have to do any rounding, because it is already rounded to the ten.

Therefore, rounded number of 635 to the nearest ten is 640.

"End"